Lorenz

Robin Hood
OF SHERWOOD FOREST

by ANN McGOVERN

Illustrated by Tracy Sugarman

SCHOLASTIC BOOK SERVICES
NEW YORK • TORONTO • LONDON • AUCKLAND • SYDNEY

Loren

For Aunt Fran

Copyright © 1968 by Ann McGovern. This edition is published
by Scholastic Book Services, a division of Scholastic Magazines,
Inc., by arrangement with Thomas Y. Crowell Company.

1st printing .... December 1968
Printed in the U.S.A.

CONTENTS

1 How Robin Hood Comes
   to Sherwood Forest   5

2 How Robin Hood Meets Little John   12

3 How Robin Hood Turns Butcher   21

4 How Little John Becomes
   the Sheriff's Servant   32

5 How the Sheriff Comes
   to Sherwood Forest   44

6 How the Sheriff Tries to Get Revenge   55

7 How Robin Hood Meets Friar Tuck   65

8 How Robin Hood Saves a Wedding   78

9 How Robin Hood Shoots for the
   Queen and Wins a Bride   93

10 How Robin Hood is Pardoned   113

1

How Robin Hood Comes to Sherwood Forest

It was a merry May morning, and Robin Hood walked with a bold heart and steps as brisk as the winds that blew through Sherwood Forest. For he was on his way to Nottingham Town, where he would test his skill alongside the Sheriff's best bowmen at Nottingham Fair.

Though this brave, stalwart youth was only seventeen, as an archer he had no peer in all of England. So Robin's hopes of winning the Sheriff's prize of a purse of gold were higher than the floating clouds in the bright May morning sky.

Strolling along, he thought of nothing but the coming contest — and of fair Marian, the young maid to whom Robin had given his heart and his pledge. He thought of how her black eyes would gleam when he handed her the prize.

Now he whistled; now he sang; now he leapt across the brook, taking care that his stout bow and score of arrows would not tumble as he ran free as the King's deer in the forest.

Then, as Robin came out of the sun-dappled woods into a mossy clearing, he came across a band of seven foresters, making merry with food and drink beneath a great tree.

Their leader wiped a bit of meat from his lips and called out to Robin, "Halloa, young chuck. Why art thou out among the woods when thou shouldst be home on thy mother's lap?"

The others laughed heartily, but Robin's blood ran hot, for he felt himself as much a man as any of them there.

"Mark well where I am going," Robin said sharply. "I'm off to the Fair to try my bow against such bold and ill-mannered knaves as thou."

"Hold thy tongue, sprite," said the head forester, who did not take kindly to Robin's sharp reply. "Try arms with us now, if thou art so certain of thy skill. A purseful of silver pennies is thine if those toy arrows should hit their mark."

"Enough said," replied Robin. "Only choose thy target."

The forester's grin was wicked. "Aye, but thou hast heeded not the rest of the wager. If thou hit *not* the mark, I'll baste thy head on both sides."

"The wager is made," cried Robin. "My head against the silver pennies."

The forester pointed to a crest in the wood, five-score yards distant, where a herd of gentle deer were grazing.

"Then pick me down the leader," said the forester.

Aghast, Robin cried, "Ye know these are the King's deer — that it is death to the man who kills one!"

"Thou art afraid then?" said the forester, notching an arrow.

Robin's answer was to bend his bow.

A twang of the bowstring, a humming of the goose feather — and the next moment the leader of the herd leaped high, then fell, and straightway blood appeared on its tawny coat.

Robin turned to the forester, triumph on his face.

"Ho!" cried the forester. "Now thou hast done

it, my sorry lad. Thy head will hang for having killed one of the King's deer."

"But 'twas thou that challenged me," cried Robin, his face flushing red as the blood on the fallen deer.

"But 'twas *thou* that let fly the arrow," said the chief forester. "Men, seize this rascal!"

"I wager the Sheriff will be pleased to see such a pretty outlaw," another forester cried.

Thereupon Robin, who had been edging closer to the thicket, turned and dashed into the wood.

Deep into the greenwood he ran, when of a sudden an arrow whizzed so close to him it drew blood from his ear. Another arrow and still another flew, but fortunately for Robin, all fell wide of their mark.

And still he ran until the angry growls of the foresters were swallowed by the trees of Sherwood Forest.

Robin sat down, his back against a strong oak tree; he was overwhelmed by bitter-sad thoughts.

"Am I doomed, then, to the life of an outlaw, forever hiding in the greenwood? And all because I killed a creature in the forest of the King — the forest that by rights belongs to the people? Aye, it is the foresters themselves who should be in my place this moment, and *I* should be on my merry way to the Fair."

Robin sank deeper into gloom as he thought of all those whom he would see no more — his cousins, his friends, and his dear love, Maid Marian, who now surely would never be allowed to see him again.

But Robin was made of hearty stuff, and his gloom soon lifted. "Fortunes such as mine that fall so low can only rise again," he said to himself.

Whereupon he chuckled. "So long as I am an outlaw, methinks I should be a worthy one. Two hundred pounds would be a fair price to set upon this lucky head," he said, stroking the place where the forester's arrow had almost put an end to him.

Of a sudden, a rustle in the thicket caused Robin to stiffen. He leaped to his feet, his bow in readiness.

Out of the woods stepped two men. At the sight of them Robin gave a glad cry, for he knew them well.

One was Midge the Miller's son, the other was Will Stutely; and each had a tale to tell of why he now called Sherwood Forest his home.

As Robin listened, his eyes hardened and anger rose within him. For as the men told their stories, he came to realize what path his fortunes must take him.

Life in those olden days was oftentimes cruel

and unjust for the good and the poor folk, who were
forced to pay large sums of money to the nobles
and the rich. High taxes, outrageous rents, and fines
made the poor even poorer, as they tried to scratch
a life out of the fields and forests.

Indeed, the laws of the rich were such that, whosoever stepped into the King's forest either to kill
a deer to keep his family from starving, or to cut
wood to keep them from freezing, was guilty of
crime; and, if caught, he could be hanged.

So it was that men, such as Robin Hood, Will
Stutely, Midge the Miller's son, and others as honest as these were now outlaws, though truly it was
the unjust laws that had made them so.

In Sherwood Forest they came to dwell, deep in
the greenwood where none could find them. There
they were safe, for a time, from the noose of the
Sheriff's hangman.

Before the year was out, a company of five-score
brave and stalwart outlawed yeomen came to Sherwood Forest and chose Robin Hood as their leader.

And as all men live better by rules, so did they
make strict ones so that they might help the
wronged and at the same time punish the wrong-
doers.

Each man who wore the Lincoln green of Robin
Hood's band willingly took these vows:

- That they would harm no innocent man working with his plow or walking in the greenwood.
- That knights and squires of good heart would be unharmed, as well as any child or woman, or any man in women's company.
- That to these they would give help, and would fight to give back that which had been cruelly taken away.
- That they would bring woe to those fat abbots and cruel nobles, and all who were unjust to the poor.
- That from these they would take all their ill-gotten gains.
- That if any man lied or said he had no money when his purse was filled with silver or gold — from this man would they help themselves generously.
- That to the evil-hearted Sheriff of Nottingham they would give no mercy.

And each man who swelled the ranks of Robin's band was true to the vows he took.

After a while much good was spoken of the outlaws by the gentle folk to whom Robin brought food, safety, or help in times of danger.

But the greedy rich and those without mercy kept a watchful eye, for they much feared Robin and his merry men in Sherwood Forest.

2

How Robin Hood Meets Little John

ONE SWEET SUMMER MORNING, when the birds of Sherwood Forest had just awakened to greet the dawn, up rose Robin Hood and called his merry men around him.

"As outlaws we have been idle too long," Robin said. "Today, perchance, I will stir up some adventure." He told his men to tarry in the greenwood, but to listen for his call — three notes upon his silver horn.

Slinging his quiver of arrows over his shoulder, Robin strode through the green glades of Sherwood Forest, a smile on his lips, thinking of this adventure and that. Not even thoughts of the Sheriff of Nottingham and all his evil ways could dim

Robin's pleasure in what might befall him upon this summer's day.

Finding himself out of the forest, he walked for a while on the road to Nottingham Town, where he amused himself by greeting the fair ladies and rosy milkmaids, the peddlers and gallant knights who journeyed along the road. The ones whom he smiled upon readily returned his greetings, for he was strong and handsome and he made a goodly sight, all clad in Lincoln green. And his deeds had made him known far and wide.

But the rich merchants he passed dared not look into his face, for they too had heard tales of Robin and his band, and what they heard was not to their liking.

After a while, finding no adventure on the road, Robin directed his steps toward a by-path. It led across a brook spanned by a bridge that was no more than a log.

No sooner had he started across than he spied a tall stranger coming from the other side. Thinking to cross first, since the log was only wide enough for one and not the other, Robin quickened his steps.

The stranger did likewise.

"Go back, ye giant fellow," Robin called cheerfully, "or I'll dampen thy great body in this stream."

The tall stranger took not a backward nor a forward step, but said, "Nay. Only to a better man than myself will I give way."

"Then give way, I say," said Robin, drawing an arrow from his quiver, "for I will soon show thee the better man. I have only to bend my bow, and this arrow will hit its mark at thy heart."

"Back, ye coward," cried the stranger. "There ye stand well armed with a longbow while I have nothing but this staff in my hand." With that, he took one step forward and raised his staff mightily.

Robin took a step back in surprise, for the stranger was at least seven feet tall — a good foot taller than Robin Hood — and his leg was in truth as thick as Robin's waist.

"No one has called me a coward yet," said Robin. "I will lay aside my bow and take myself a staff. Then shall we see if thou art as strong as thy words."

Whereupon the outlaw jumped nimbly into the thicket, put aside his longbow and arrows, and cut a stout oaken staff. Then back he came upon the log bridge and took his stand before the tall fellow.

"Set to!" cried Robin. "Can ye test my mettle and live to tell of it?"

The birds flew off at the great shout that arose

from the stranger as he whirled his staff over his head.

He smote Robin a blow that made his bones sing. It was well that Robin was nimble of foot; such a lusty crack would surely have caused another to lose his balance and fall into the stream.

In return, Robin hit the stranger a stinging stroke. Then their staffs flew like lightning for many minutes, and both caught blows from rib to crown that would have felled three lesser men. But neither would cry "Stop!" and neither one could knock the other off the log into the stream below.

For half an hour or more, each stood his place firmly, giving and taking whacks and cracks.

Then Robin caught the stranger a blow that made that stout man's head ring. The tall man was thrown off balance, tilting from one side to the other. The log twisted and slipped as he fought to regain his footing. Robin took a deep breath, thinking to strike another blow and so end the merry fight, when the stranger righted himself and swung heavily, fetching Robin such a clout on the head that he fell headlong into the stream.

"Forsooth," called Robin, splashing and sputtering, "thou art the best hand with a staff in all Nottingham."

"Aye, the best in all of England," cried the winner, laughing at the sight of Robin, who was trying to catch hold of some slippery weeds along the banks of the stream.

"Marry yes, in all of the world, ye great lout," Robin sputtered. "Enough talk, I say. Lend me a hand, for the cold water soaks my bones."

Whereupon the stranger stretched down his staff into the water. Robin laid hold of it, and the stranger pulled him out as if he were but a small fish.

For a time Robin lay upon the sun-warmed grass until he could regain his full senses. Then, reaching for his silver horn, he blew three clear notes.

Scarcely had the echo of the call died away in the glade when came a score of good stout men, all clothed in Lincoln green.

"Master Robin!" cried Will Stutely, eyeing the tall stranger darkly. "Thou art as wet as raindrops. How is this?"

"This stout fellow gave my ribs a cracking they shall not soon forget, and tumbled me into the stream as well," replied Robin.

"A plague on him!" Will cried. "Now shall he have a ducking as large as his size. Seize him, lads."

Robin's eyes twinkled as he commanded. "Nay. Do not harm him. The fight was brave and fair."

Turning to the stranger, he held out his hand. "Thou art a stout fellow and will come to no harm. These lads are my loyal bowmen. Come join us and live thy life among the finest fellows ye have ever known. Three suits of Lincoln green shall ye have for thy service and forty pieces of gold besides. What say ye?"

"I do not give my service easily to any man, sir," said the stranger. "Furthermore, if thy skill with bow and arrows is equal to thy skill with the staff, I will fast follow the road away from here."

"Ho," laughed Robin. "Thou art as cocky as thou art large." He ordered his men to pin a mark as big as a hand upon a great oak tree some fourscore yards away. Next he ordered a bow for the stranger and a fine gray goose shaft.

"Now by my faith," said Robin, "if thou canst hit that mark, I shall call thee a true archer."

Not a word did the stranger say, but notching an arrow to the string of the bow, he sent it humming to the very centre of the mark.

A great cheer came from the merry men, and Will Stutely cried, "Huzzah! I know only one man who can shoot so well."

Then Robin took up his own bow and said, "A noble shot, stranger. Indeed I cannot do better, but perchance I may dislodge your shaft from the mark itself."

Without so much as pausing to take aim, he loosed his shaft, and the only sound was the whirring of the arrow until it split the stranger's shaft to splinters.

Then all the yeomen cheered their master, but the stranger cheered loudest of all.

"Never in all the songs that are sung have I heard of a finer shot than this," he said. "Truly thou art my better, and I am honoured to have a place among thy merry men."

"Gaining a good man this day was well worth drinking the fish's water," laughed Robin. "But tell me thy name, stranger."

"John Little is what I am called in my own country," the stranger said.

Will Stutely laughed and said, "Fair little fellow, thy name fits thee not. With a twist here and there, ye shall be better named—Little John."

At this, all the merry men roared with laughter, and Little John could not help but laugh with them.

"Henceforth shall ye be Little John and my right-hand man, and a merry feast shall there be to welcome thee," said Robin Hood.

With Robin leading the way, they all strode into

the forest to the place deep in the greenwood where
they dwelt.

There they found the rest of the band, some of
whom had just returned from hunting, with a brace
of fat does.

Soon the fires were blazing and a barrel of ale
stood ready.

With Robin at the centre of the board, Will
Stutely at one side and Little John on the other,
there was much singing of songs and feasting that
night. With true merriment, all drank to the health
of the new member of the band till the barrel stood
empty and the moon rose to replace the light of the
sun.

But before the merry men went to their leafy
beds in the greenwood, all joined hands and made
a ring about Little John and Robin Hood. Then
loud and long did they cheer the tall yeoman and
their beloved master.

Thus it was that Robin Hood gained a dunking
in the stream and a loyal man and true, all in the
same day.

3

How Robin Hood Turns Butcher

FOR A TIME AFTER Little John joined Robin Hood's band, the outlaws lived an easy pleasant life in the greenwood. They spent the full summer months testing their skill and strength at shooting, wrestling, and merry bouts with the quarterstaff.

But the day came when Robin Hood yearned for the high road and adventure. He called Little John to him and said, " 'Tis a good day to fetch a guest to dine at our board."

At this, Little John laughed loudly, for he had heard Robin tell stories about the rich merchants and noblemen who were brought to the greenwood as guests, then sent on their way with full bellies but empty purses.

"I'd like a chance at that sport," said Little John. "I may topple the rest of the yeomen at quarter-staff or shoot the King's deer at a distance of eighty yards, but I have yet to master the fine art of give-and-take." He laughed heartily, saying, "That is, giving to the poor that which we take from the rich."

"Good Little John," said Robin, laughing with him. "Thou art my right hand, and to show that I think thee worthy of that title, I will make thee a wager. Three silver pennies are thine if thou hast a better adventure than I, this day."

Little John readily agreed, and so it was they left the leafy shelter of the greenwood and travelled on the high road to Nottingham Town.

At the wide fork in the road, they bade each other farewell. Little John turned to the left and Robin to the right, each believing in his heart that he would outdo the other in merry sport.

What befell Little John we shall hear in due time. Let us begin with Robin Hood's tale.

Robin had not gone very far when he heard a creaking of wooden wheels. At the sight of a stout butcher driving a cart laden with meats, a bold plan crossed his mind.

"Good morrow, friend," called Robin stepping

in front of the butcher's cart. "I pray thee stop but a moment or two."

"Prithee, fair fellow," the butcher replied, "methinks ye give me no choice, else my old mare will flatten thee in the road. Pray, do not keep me too long from my business."

"What is now thy business may soon be mine," said Robin, his eyes all atwinkle.

"Who art thou, knave, to be so bold with other people's business? In my country, a stout butcher like myself does not listen kindly to such remarks as ye have just made."

"Peace, brother," said Robin Hood. " 'Tis easily seen that in any country thou art a stalwart knave. As for my name, know that thou speakest to Robin Hood."

"Mercy," cried the butcher in terror. "I have heard of thee, Robin Hood, and of thy bold band who rob openly on the King's high road. But I am only a poor butcher on his way to Nottingham Town to earn an honest penny."

"Tremble not, my friend," said Robin. "If truly ye know of me, ye should well know that the poor and honest have nothing to fear from the likes of us."

"Then let me be on my way," said the butcher, still pale.

"One moment more," laughed Robin. "To prove the truth of what I say, I would gladly strike a fair bargain with thee. Tell me, what is the best price thou canst fetch for this old cart, tired mare, and all thy goodly meat?"

The butcher thought hard, for he was an honest man and fain would not cheat anyone, much less the bold man in Lincoln green who stood before him.

Finally he answered, "Ten gold pieces would be fair."

Whereupon Robin drew forth a purse heavy with coin.

"Done!" he exclaimed. "Ye'll find ten gold pieces — and more besides."

"May the heavens bless thee, good Robin Hood," said the butcher joyfully.

"One more request and this the last," said Robin. "If thou wilt trade thy butcher's garb for this suit of Lincoln green, I will add still another gold coin."

So the trade was made, and the butcher waved good-bye, a handsome suit on his back, a heavy purse at his girdle, and a puzzled frown on his face, for he knew not why Robin Hood chose to be — of all things — a butcher.

Whistling a merry tune, Robin drove the mare and the heavy cart to the butchers' square in the market of Nottingham Town. Most of the stalls were already filled, so Robin had to take a place near the end. As he wended his way, he called out, "Ho, fair lasses, good wives, gentle dames. Follow me; follow, follow, follow me. Here is the reddest beef, the sweetest lamb, the whitest veal, the fattest mutton, the likes of which ye have never seen."

Then all around looked at the young butcher, for they had never seen one handsomer. And the next words he cried made some stare and others roar with laughter, for thus he spoke: "My prices are wondrous fair. Fat abbots and rich noblemen who buy from me must pay double, for I want not their trade. But honest men, poor widows, and gentle folk may have three pennyworths of meat for one penny only. And bonny lasses have the best bargain. To them I will charge naught but a kiss. So follow me; follow, follow, follow me."

Follow him they did—the good wives and widows who got more than they paid for, and the fair lasses who were drawn to his stall, not so much for his good meat but for his bold manner and blue eyes and a kiss from his merry lips.

Soon the last mutton chop was sold in Robin Hood's stall, and the other butchers started to grumble amongst themselves, for their stalls were still well filled with meat.

Some said, "He must be a thief who has stolen a poor butcher's cart and wares."

"Nay," the others argued. "Whoever heard of a thief who would give his money freely?"

Another said, "Methinks he must be a rich man's son without a care, who would laugh his money away to the last penny."

And so they argued and wondered about the stranger until one of the butchers said, "I mean to find out more. For whoever this knave is, perchance we could learn from him."

So saying, he went up to Robin Hood and greeted him thus: "Thou hast had good fortune this day, friend. Now wouldst thou like to see good times this night?"

"Merry sport is my middle name," Robin laughed. "What is thy game?"

"Feasting, good sir," the butcher replied. "Come with us to the banquet hall. Tonight the Sheriff of Nottingham is holding a feast for all the butchers. Since it is well known that our Sheriff dearly loves a good table, the fare is sure to be of thy liking."

"Agreed, and gladly," Robin Hood said, for he would like nothing better than to meet his enemy face to face. To himself, he said, "Tonight Little John will surely lose our wager, for what could be

better adventure than to make a fool of the Sheriff
— if more of a fool he can be made to be."

A goodly crowd was already assembled when
Robin Hood joined the company of butchers in
the Sheriff's great hall. The Sheriff had heard tidings of the newcomer who dribbled away money
like water. Since no man in all of England liked gold
and silver more than the Sheriff, he thought to make
much of the handsome stranger. He said to himself,
"Why should I not reap the benefits of a fool's generosity?" And knowing him not in his butcher's
garb, he bade Robin sit at his right hand. At each
of Robin's merry jests, the Sheriff laughed loudest,
for he was eager to gain the lad's favour.

After much laughter and song, the serving men
brought in platters laden with roasted meats and
fowl on silver skewers, thick brown bread, and gob-
lets brimming with red wine. Whereupon Robin
sprang from his seat, raised his glass, and cried,
"For such a goodly feast and stout company, I toast
our host. Be carefree, knaves, and spare not meat
nor drink. For this board and all upon it I will pay,
though it cost me my purse."

Thereupon all the butchers rose, and the great
hall echoed with their lusty cheers.

"Thou art a merry blade," said the Sheriff.

"Surely thou hast many head of horned beasts and much rich land, to spend thy gold so freely."

Robin replied, "Truly, my brothers and I have five hundred and ten horned beasts, and none can we sell, which is why thou seest me in butcher's clothes. As for my land, it is too wide to count the acres."

Hearing this, the Sheriff's eyes gleamed with greed. Lowering his voice so none could hear, he said, "How much are thy cattle worth? Perchance I could help thee find a buyer for them?"

"Dost thou think three hundred gold pieces too much to ask for them?" Robin said, feigning innocence.

"Three hundred!" the Sheriff sputtered, nearly choking on his meat at the ridiculously low price Robin had quoted.

"Then thou thinkest the price high," said Robin, pretending to misunderstand.

"Aye, 'tis high," said the Sheriff slowly, knowing in his heart that the cattle were worth twice as much. "But I have taken a strong liking to thee, and fain would I help thee in thy plight. I myself will buy from thee, albeit the price is high." Then the Sheriff spoke softly lest some honest butcher should take Robin to task for selling so cheap. "Let's settle the matter at once. Hard silver and gold will I pay if thou deliverest the beasts to me on the morrow."

"Nay, that I cannot do," said Robin, "for they scatter as they graze over my wide lands. But thou mayest come to see them and choose the best for thy keeping. 'Tis only an hour's ride from here at most."

"'Tis late for such a journey," said the Sheriff, "and in the darkness I may miss a prize. If thou wilt lead me to thy lands on the morrow, gladly shall I give thee a bed this night."

Now tricking an enemy is one thing, Robin thought, but sharing his house overnight is another. He liked not the Sheriff's plan, but taking care not to rouse his suspicion, he thanked the Sheriff and accepted, pretending gladness all the while.

Pleased that the matter was so easily settled and dreaming of the gold that would clink in his purse, the Sheriff called out, "Ho! More drink for our honoured guest. Where is my new serving man, Reynold Greenleaf?" He turned to Robin and said, "No stouter man wilt thou ever see than the man who donned my colours this very day and promised to serve me faithfully. Why, his arm is as wide as the stoutest timber in this hall."

Whereupon he bellowed, "Reynold Greenleaf! Come hither and bring drink to my guest."

Robin turned eagerly to see who this bold knave

might be. He nearly dropped his goblet when he spied none other than Little John. Little John was no less surprised to see his master dressed in butcher's garb. But they quickly hid the laughter that threatened to bubble from their lips.

"Ye spoke fair," Robin said to the Sheriff. "A stouter lad, truly, I have never seen."

A frown appeared upon the Sheriff's brow as he said, "Methinks if I should ever do battle with that villain Robin Hood, my man Greenleaf would crack the scoundrel's skull."

"Thy man looks as strong as a giant oak indeed," said Robin, "but I have heard tale of the right-hand man in Robin Hood's band called Little John who, they say, can flatten any man with but one stroke of his quarterstaff."

The Sheriff, wishing to put an end to such unpleasant talk, rose to depart. "Lay thy head down at an early hour," he told Robin Hood. "I am eager to have an early start to see those great beasts on the morrow."

As soon as the Sheriff had left the hall, Little John came to where Robin was sitting, and while filling his goblet, leaned down and whispered in his ear, "Come see me in the kitchen, master, for I have a story to tell which will bring forth laughter from thee for many a month."

4

How Little John Becomes the Sheriff's Servant

Being certain that none noticed his leave-taking, Robin Hood slipped away from the great hall and made his way to the kitchen to seek Little John.

Had Robin but known what trouble Little John was in at that very moment, he would have hastened his steps.

For that tall knave, having naught to eat for many an hour, was asking the Sheriff's steward for some food.

"Good sir steward," he begged, "a little venison pasty, if it please thee, and some cool ale to wash it down."

"Begone," said the steward, for he was jealous

of the favours the Sheriff had bestowed upon this new serving man. "Thou art a fool, Reynold Greenleaf, to think that I would unlock the pantry at this hour." And he rattled the pantry keys before Little John's nose. "Take thine hunger, and to bed with thee."

"I'd rather crack thy fat crown," Little John replied in anger.

The steward, noting how red in the face Little John was growing, took a fast accounting of the breadth and width of his foe, and started for the door.

But for all of his size, Little John was fleet of foot, and before the steward could open the door, Little John smote him such a blow that even Robin Hood, hiding behind the velvet draperies, could hear the crack.

The steward groaned and rolled on the floor, thinking to rise. But with his head still ringing, he remained where he was.

Little John seized the steward's keys, opened the pantry door, and helped himself to wine, meat, and bread.

"I drink to thy health," said Little John, "even if thou wilt not drink with me."

Robin Hood was almost doubled over with

laughter at what had gone on. He was about to enter the kitchen when he heard footsteps coming
down the hall.

Again he hid behind the draperies till he heard
Little John exclaim, "How now, good sir cook! Join
me in feasting on the very foods thou hast prepared.
This venison pasty is fit for a king, and I swear this
ale the best that ever wet thy lips. Step over that
bundle of fat rags lying there on the floor and set
to."

Now the cook was stronger in body and braver
in heart than the steward, and so he feared not
Little John.

"What manner of man art thou, Reynold Greenleaf, to win our master's favour and then help thyself
to his food and drink?" Whereupon he dealt Little
John three bold strokes with his staff.

Smarting with the sting, Little John raised his
own quarterstaff, saying, "Truly thou art a brave
soul to come between me and my feast, and those
clouts nearly did away with my appetite. But let
us see whether this will bring it back." And Little
John thought to give back to the cook in blows that
which he had received.

The cook raised his staff and so did Little John,
and there in the pantry they exchanged blows, staff
against staff.

To Robin Hood, listening outside, they sounded like two Sherwood stags locked in combat.

So busy were they in battle, that neither noticed when Robin Hood stepped through the door. Robin was curious to see who would be the victor, for the cook seemed as large in size as his right-hand man. But he saw neither a victor nor a loser, for so skillfully did they parry each other's blows that neither did harm to the other. As soon as one shouted, "Ye vile knave," the other roared, "Ye villain lout."

Then Little John swung and missed again, shouting, "Thy name may be cook, but I'll make better mincemeat of thee than thou couldst in thy own kitchen."

The cook swung, and likewise missing, cried, "Aye, cook I am, and I'll show all seven tall feet of thee that I can baste thy head as well as I baste my roasts."

Then Robin saw that both men were beginning to fight with shortened breath, so he stepped between them. Laughing, he said, "Never have I seen such lusty knaves. Methinks ye would rather eat a pasty and drink together than crack heads and break bones."

At that, both men dropped their staffs willingly. The steward, who had been hiding under the table

during the bout, saw that the climate of the room had changed, and without stopping to make the acquaintance of Robin Hood, bid a hasty retreat.

The cook, now jolly, laughed and said, "Since I cannot fight ye both, I'll feed ye till I hear 'Stop!'" Away he went, returning in a twinkling with a large platter of cold pheasant and the Sheriff's best wine.

The three ate and drank with much merriment. Then Robin turned to the cook and said, "Now that we love one another well, it is time ye know us by our rightful names. This knave ye call Reynold Greenleaf is known in Sherwood Forest by the

name of Little John. As for myself, these butcher's clothes cover Robin Hood."

The cook, dropping his meat and sputtering on a mouthful of wine, cried, "Mercy, I beg thee. Thy name is hated in this place. Let me go in peace, and I swear the Sheriff will not hear of Little John nor Robin Hood from my lips."

"Hold, good cook," Robin said, laughing. "Thou hast naught to fear. By my faith, thou art so strong with the quarterstaff and so nimble with thy pots and pans that, if thou art willing, thou shouldst leave the Sheriff's house and come live a joyous life in Sherwood Forest. Thou wilt have finer food and sweeter drink than ever the Sheriff laid upon the table. Forty gold coins will be thy pay and two suits of Lincoln green besides. What sayest thou?"

"Right gladly do I say aye," cried the cook happily, and raising his goblet, said, "I drink to thee, and by my troth, I swear I will serve thee faithfully and well."

Then Robin Hood told his companions how he came to be in butcher's clothes and all about his bold scheme to trick the Sheriff on the morrow.

"And now, what of thee, Little John?" Robin asked. "What hath come to pass since we parted on the road early this morn?"

"Eager to have a better adventure than thee, good master, I set out for the Fair at Nottingham Town," Little John began. "I thought to bring home proof of my adventures in the form of a prize captured in wrestling, or in shooting with the longbow, or perchance at a bout with the quarterstaff.

"The Fair was right merry. The minstrels sang like nightingales, and the lasses, I wot, were the fairest I ever did see in all of England. Many a turn I danced with them before I went to seek stronger sport.

"I came to a wooden platform where stood a lusty fellow swinging a great staff and shouting at the crowd below in this manner: 'Are all yeomen of Nottingham such cowards that none will come forward and have a merry bout with me?'

"I asked who the saucy knave was and learned his name — Eric of Lincoln; and his fame — cracking the crown of anyone who took up staff against him.

"Then he spied me amid the others, for well ye know that I stand a full head and shoulders above most men and am hard to hide. The braggart shouted for all to hear, 'Thy legs are long, thy shoulders broad, but thy courage must indeed be tiny.'

"Now much did I want to keep my head smooth and free from cracks, but I do not take kindly to the name of coward. So without a word, I leapt upon the platform while the crowd cheered.

"Seeing Eric of Lincoln at close range, I knew he could send me spinning if my skill should fault me for an instant. So standing firm guard, I started boldly and fetched the braggart a sound buffet on the shoulder. Then, as swift as a humming bird, did he whack my ribs. And so began the bout that people said later was the finest that e'er took place in Nottingham Town.

"Right deftly we stroked and parried, and so well matched were we that neither could smite the other the winning blow.

"Soon Eric grew angry and began to strike with such force that his blows made thunderclaps sound like sneezes. But I parried his strokes well, and at the same time, looked for a way to send his staff to kingdom come. When I saw the chance I seized it, striking a blow on Eric's back, and then right speedily a blow to his ribs, and then a stinging blow on his crown. His staff flew into the air, and he fell to the platform floor like a sack of flour.

"So loud were the cheers that people left the booths from all sides of the Fair and came running to see what the clamour was all about.

"And then one man came up, and as all around doffed their caps, I guessed he was a person of some importance. I quickly learned he was none other than our enemy—the Sheriff of Nottingham. He shook my hand and said, 'Thou art the stoutest fellow my eyes ever beheld, and truly I would like to see thee in my service.'

"I thought to myself, 'Ho! Gladly will I accept to see what mischief I can do. Then surely I shall win our wager.'

"But not wanting to appear too eager, I said, 'My name is Reynold Greenleaf, and Reynold Greenleaf is worth a goodly pay. What have ye to offer?'

"The Sheriff, not liking to open his purse wider than he had to, said, 'Thou shalt have good food to eat, sweet wine to drink, and fine clothes to put upon thy strong back.'

"'And the pay?' I asked again, enjoying his squirmings.

"Then the Sheriff said, 'Twenty gold coins,' but in such a low voice that none could bear witness to his promise.

"After a while, the prize to the winner was announced, and, good master, ye will laugh to hear what it was, for we have better in our own greenwood. Two fat steers did I get for my trouble. I angered the Sheriff straight off, for I offered to give the steers to the good people at the Fair, and he had thought to make his table heavy with my prize.

"But I cared not for his anger, and all the way to this place I laughed at my first trick and thought up others. And much is the trouble I have caused since I came here.

"So, fair master, what think ye of my adventure? Do I win the wager?"

Robin Hood and the cook could hardly stop laughing at Little John's tale. Then Robin said, "Let the cook be the judge, for he has heard both our stories. What say, fair fellow? Who has had the best adventure?"

The cook, still laughing, said, "I swear I cannot tell. One man turns butcher; the other, servant; and both come to the same place to play merry pranks on that villain, my former master!"

"Nay, ye must declare a winner," Little John said.

So the cook thought harder and at last said, "Aye, I know well who it may be. No one but myself! Truly the best adventure is mine, for soon I leave this place to make my merry life in Sherwood Forest. And to keep alive the memory of my former master, I shall take with me the Sheriff's finest plates and silver — all I can carry."

"Ho for thee, jolly cook," said Robin, taking from

his purse three silver pennies. "Right gladly do I give these to thee. Now leave the Sheriff's house with his booty before thou art discovered. And, Little John, do likewise. Tomorrow we three shall meet in the greenwood. Tell our men to make ready a wondrous feast for our guest—the Sheriff of Nottingham."

And so once more Little John and Robin Hood said their farewells, but this time Little John had the company of the cook and the promise of more adventure on the morrow.

5

How the Sheriff Comes
to Sherwood Forest

THE NEXT MORNING Robin Hood slept overlong, since he was used to being awakened by the sweet birds in Sherwood Forest.

But thoughts of the great prank he would play upon his enemy this fine day caused him to leap from his pallet. For the last time he dressed in his butcher clothes, and whistling a merry tune, went down to breakfast in the great hall.

"Ho, my sweet man of meat," cried the Sheriff in greeting. "Sit thee down to feast on fresh kidneys and ale, though they are not their usual best. My cook was not in the kitchen this morning, which puzzleth me, and my steward lies abed groaning."

Robin tried to hide the smile on his lips while the Sheriff continued, "But thou needest not concern thyself with matters of my household. Let us be off to see thy herd of horned beasts. Thou hast not forgotten thy promise to sell?"

"My memory is as sharp as the sword ye carry, good Sheriff," said Robin Hood. "I remember it as well as I remember thy promise of three hundred gold coins in payment."

"It has been counted thrice, and I have just sent for five stout men to guard us along the way to where thy cattle graze. Truly we will be safe with men such as Reynold Greenleaf by our side."

Robin nearly choked when he heard that name, and he said quickly, "Let us tarry not a moment longer. The sun will soon be high. As for thy guards, there is no need where I take thee."

"But hold," cried the Sheriff, giving voice to his inmost fear. "Thy lands lie near the greenwood home of that great villain, Robin Hood. What if the rogue should rob us both?"

"Fear not," Robin Hood said, "for that outlaw hath promised me safe passage through his country in return for a favour I once did him. Let us begin our journey forthwith, so that thou mayest get thy herd home by nightfall."

Greed overcame fear, and the Sheriff called for his swiftest horse to be made ready. So they left the great house, the Sheriff riding and Robin running alongside. On the way Robin passed the time by recounting this story and that about how Robin Hood robbed the rich and gave to the poor. The very tales that delighted Robin made the Sheriff grow pale under his beard.

By and by the two were deep in the forest glade. The more they travelled, the more fearful the Sheriff became. He peered right and left into the shadowy thicket and listened hard for any sudden snapping of a twig that would mean the outlaws were nigh.

Of a sudden, Robin Hood led the way to a narrow path. Then cried the Sheriff, "Where art thou taking me?"

But Robin merely laughed and said, "Why, good Sheriff, dost thou have so little trust in me? I and my brothers keep the cattle yonder." And he pointed to a sunlit clearing where stood several dozen of the King's deer peacefully grazing.

"What thou seest here is only a portion of my herd," said Robin. "How dost thou like my horned beasts?"

The Sheriff, now knowing that a trick had been played upon him, drew rein sharply and cried out,

"Vile butcher, I no longer care to see thy herd. The bargain is off! Go thy way, and I will go mine."

At this, Robin gave a gleeful laugh and held fast to the Sheriff's bridle rein.

"Nay, nay, good Sheriff, a bargain is a bargain. Prithee stay a while, for I would have thee meet my brothers." Whereupon he drew forth from under his butcher's apron the silver bugle-horn and blew three clear blasts.

The deer scattered in all directions as the echoing notes brought a score of men running, all dressed in Lincoln green, with Little John in the lead.

"How now, Sheriff," said Little John, "thou must miss me sorely to come all this way just to gaze upon my face."

At the sight of the man he knew as Reynold Greenleaf, the Sheriff flew into such a rage that he sputtered and stammered.

" 'Tis thine own fault that I left thy service," Little John said. "I was nigh starved at thy house. And thy pay doth not compare with what this good master gives." Doffing his cap, he bowed before Robin Hood.

Then the Sheriff turned to Robin Hood. "Thou hast lied to me, villain," he said, "for thou didst swear we would be in no danger."

Robin replied, "Aye, that is so. Truly thou art in no danger in these glades. For I know these men well and call them brothers, just as they call me Robin Hood."

The Sheriff spoke not another word, for fear made his tongue silent.

"Ho, good Sheriff," Robin laughed. "This is no day for gloom. Thou hast feasted me in thy house, and now in the greenwood I mean to show thee our favours."

Then Little John laid a blindfold across the Sheriff's eyes, and taking his bridle rein in hand, led

the Sheriff down this path and that till they came to
where the tall oak stood.

Already bright fires were crackling, and good
smells of roasting venison filled the greenwood.

"While thy dinner cooks, good Sheriff," Robin
said, taking off the man's blindfold, "let us have
entertainment in thine honour."

Though he had been sorely afraid, the Sheriff
now began to take heart, since none had spoken of
the coins that clinked in his purse; and, as he
watched the merry games that took place before his
eyes, he began to enjoy his stay, forgetting for the
moment where he was.

He saw archers who loosed their gray goose
shafts and pierced willow wands at ninety paces.
He saw merry men playing at quarterstaff with
such strokes and parries that he cried out, "Well
struck, fellows."

He saw wrestlers who could have cracked the
backbone of Eric of Lincoln, and men who outran
the King's deer and pulled them down by their
horns.

After each man in Robin's band had taken his
turn, Robin turned to the Sheriff and said, "Dost
think ye can draw an arrow with any here? If ye
can, then shall we give thee thy feast for naught.
But if ye fail, ye shall take a buffet from Little John

— or, as ye are wont to call him, Reynold Green-leaf!"

At Robin's words the Sheriff trembled, for today he had seen such bold men as to put the King's own to shame at the tourneys.

He looked about him and spied a small page who seemed no taller than a new-born fawn. Thereupon he said, "Here is the one I will shoot with."

Robin laughed and said to the youth, "Make a mark for thyself and the good Sheriff." So the lad placed a garland of flowers some eighty yards distant.

"Surely, thou jestest," the Sheriff said, for he thought the boy a mere stripling. "Thou canst not send thine arrows half that distance, much less hit the mark."

Robin said never a word but handed the Sheriff his finest bow and shaft. Although the Sheriff shot fairly, nowhere did he come near the mark.

"Come, lad," laughed Robin Hood, "show our guest what life in the greenwood hast taught thee."

The boy, who barely stood as high as the Sheriff's chest, drew back his bow and sent as pretty a shot as the Sheriff e'er saw — straight to the mark. Then he loosed another shaft and sent it spinning so that it splintered the first.

Then the Sheriff could not help but wonder if he

would leave the forest with his life as well as his purse.

"Hold," Robin cried to Little John who was approaching to give the Sheriff his due. "There is another here who would welcome this chance above all others."

Thereupon he gave a signal and up ran the cook. Then did the Sheriff cry in rage, "Thou good-for-nothing varlet, thou villain. I'll see thee hanged if thou art not back in Nottingham this night."

Laughing, the cook said, "I'd as soon see myself hanged as spend one more night in thy service. Here's payment for the years I've spent with thee!" And he fetched the Sheriff such a clout that down he went to the ground and did not stir till Little John roused him with a dash of ale in his face.

"Nay," cried Robin Hood. "Is that a fair way to treat our guest? Up, good Sheriff. The cloth is spread upon the green grass, and a feast of sweet venison, rich brown pasties, and the finest English ale await thee."

Then when the Sheriff saw that he was served with his own silver plates, he was almost beside himself with rage.

But when Robin called forth his best musician, who made much sweet music, the Sheriff ate as heartily as Robin's own men. And as the day grew shorter so his hopes grew stronger that he would escape with his purse untouched.

When the moon was high, the Sheriff rose and said, "I thank thee for all the high entertainment thou hast shown me this day. And I forgive thee, Cook. The fine foods thou hast set before me truly amend for the buffeting thou gavest me. Now bold Robin Hood, may I have my horse?"

Robin turned to Will Stutely and said, "Fetch the Sheriff's horse and help him find his way upon the road to Nottingham."

The fires burned low, and Robin raised his glass, saying, "Let us give three cheers for the Sheriff. One for his silver plates, one for his cook, and one for his three hundred gold coins."

While all stood about and cheered heartily, the Sheriff's heart sank, for above all he had wished to leave with his money.

When Robin had the Sheriff's purse in his hand and the coins were clinking into tall piles, he cried, "Another cheer for our good Sheriff, for he is truly a generous fellow."

The cheer echoed through the greenwood as the Sheriff clenched his fist in anger.

"And now," said Robin. "Fare thee well, honoured guest. Go home to thy great house and thy soft bed. Take with thee thy silver plates, for we are not used to such finery in our simple life."

So once more the blindfold was placed over the Sheriff's eyes, and as he was led out of Sherwood Forest, he rued the day he had first heard of Robin Hood. Listening to the clank of his silver plates with each step his horse travelled, the Sheriff plotted how he would get sweet revenge.

6

How the Sheriff Tries to Get Revenge

ALL THE WAY HOME from Sherwood Forest and
the next day and the day after that, the Sheriff
thought of nothing but how to take revenge on
Robin Hood. The more he thought, the angrier he
became until he could neither eat nor sleep.

One cool September night he lay abed for many
hours without closing his eyes. At last he decided
on a scheme to trap Robin Hood within the gates
of Nottingham Town — and then to hang him! By
the time the sun paled the sky, the Sheriff had
worked out his plan in every detail.

Early in the morning threescore of the Sheriff's
horsemen rode far and wide into the countryside,

proclaiming a shooting contest that was to take place in a fortnight. Every man who could hold a bow was bidden to shoot for the prize of a silver arrow tipped with a head of purest gold.

In a short time tidings of this match came to the greenwood.

The Robin Hood called his merry men about him. "The Sheriff's proclamation has a smell about it as bad as a barrel of stale ale," he said. "If he thinks to make us fools — dead fools at that — the more fool he! But hearken to this cunning" — whereupon Robin spoke his plan:

The best archers of the band would go thither to Nottingham Town, with Robin himself among them, to shoot for the prize.

Each would change the colour of his hair and beard with dyes made from berries and bark in the woods.

Each would dress in a mantle of coloured cloth, some in rags like beggars, to hide the cloth of Lincoln green beneath.

A score of other bold men would make their way among the crowd, their best bows and arrows hidden beneath their cloaks, lest there be trouble.

When the day of the match dawned bright and clear, a strange band of men made their way along

the high road to Nottingham Town. Some were
dressed in rags and shreds, like beggars; other wore
bright-coloured cloaks. But the strangest by far was
the man who led them. All in scarlet was he, and not
even his limping walk nor the black patch that covered his right eye could hide his bold, handsome
air.

The fairgrounds of Nottingham Town had never
looked gayer. From the striped tents and peddlers'
stalls, many-coloured ribbons fluttered in the mild
autumn breeze.

The sounds that filled the air were holiday sounds
— minstrels singing of heroes and heartbreak; rosy-
cheeked lasses laughing as they danced to the
music of fiddle and fife; peddlers shouting their
wares; silver bells tinkling on carts and horses.

But if one cared to listen well, one name could be
heard over and over — the name of Robin Hood.
For most of the people in this part of the country
had heard of the many ways in which Robin had
tricked the Sheriff, and they knew the true reason
for the shooting match. In their heart of hearts, the
good poor folk hoped Robin Hood would stay safely
away this day. But the rich and powerful longed for
his capture.

And, in truth, the Sheriff and his men-at-arms
feared that Robin Hood had stayed away. No man

in Lincoln green could be seen in the crowd, or for that matter, anyone who came near to fitting Robin Hood's description.

Now the crowd spilled over onto the green, where the match was soon to take place. The Sheriff and his lady sat in the centre of the stands reserved for squires, abbots, rich knights and their ladies. The poor folk stayed behind a wooden rail built to keep them away from the targets.

All was still for a moment as the heralds raised their trumpets to their lips to announce that the match was beginning and to give the rules.

Then heads turned and eyes peered as the archers took their places — eight hundred in all. Plucking at his beard nervously, the Sheriff studied each archer who made his try with the arrow. "Many beggars and fools are here today," he thought, "but by my faith, none that wears the face of Robin Hood."

At first each man was allowed to shoot only one arrow. Those who came closest to the mark could shoot again — and this was repeated over and over until the contest narrowed down to ten men.

"If Robin Hood is here," thought the Sheriff, "he will be shooting now, for only the noblest arms are left." And he signalled to his guardsmen to be wary and watchful of those they did not know.

Of the ten, the Sheriff and most of the company present recognized six — famous throughout the land for their bold shooting. The Sheriff said to himself, "Of the four strangers, none has a beard like Robin's — yellow as the sun — and only the crippled beggar stands as tall as that villainous outlaw. But hold . . . something about him . . . but no, how can I seize a one-eyed cripple and claim he is Robin Hood? If I were to be wrong, the people would laugh me out of this country." So went the Sheriff's thoughts as, one by one, the remaining men shot at the mark. So wondrous was their skill that not a word was spoken in all the watching throng.

Now the contest was between two men — the one-eyed and crippled beggar, dressed all in red, and a tall fellow wearing a blue cloak.

There were pleased murmurs among the archers who had shot earlier but had failed to top the skill of the two men on the green. And no wonder, for these two who now raised their bows were none other than Will Stutely and Robin Hood!

First it was Robin's turn. He limped to the line and almost carelessly sped the shaft. Fair flew his arrow and lit a hair's breath from the target's centre.

"A Scarlet! A Scarlet!" cheered the crowd for the tattered stranger in red.

Next to shoot was Will. With a flourish he raised his arm high to draw back his bow. In doing so, his cloak parted to reveal the Lincoln green colour of the outlaw band.

At this, the Sheriff, getting on his feet, shouted to his guardsmen, "Seize him! Seize the villain! Death to any of Robin Hood's men!"

Then forty of Robin's men looked to their red-clad leader to spring into action. But Robin would not move a muscle, even when twelve men-at-arms dragged Will Stutely from the green.

The Sheriff's heralds blew upon their trumpets to quiet the uproarious crowd. And from the one-eyed crippled beggar in red came these words, clearly heard:

"Am I not to get the chance to draw my yew bow once again? Or is this shooting contest merely a trap to catch a wretched outlaw?"

At this, the Sheriff roared with laughter, for he was in good humour now that one of Robin Hood's men was firmly bound, although he would have liked it much better had the ties been drawn over the chest of Robin Hood himself.

"Good beggar," the Sheriff cried, "whoever thou

art, if thou shootest shrewder than the outlaw, I will add to the prize of the silver arrow fifty gold coins."

Once more Robin made ready, then loosed the string. A moment later, a gray goose feather quivered and held in the very centre of the mark.

A hush came over the crowd, followed by a great roar, for truly no one had ever seen such shooting before.

The Sheriff, still beside himself with delight, shouted so all could hear, "By my faith, thou hast shot fairer than that coward Robin Hood who dared not show his face here today but sent instead a lesser man."

At this, Robin's lips tightened and his eyes narrowed, but he made no outward sign that the words of the Sheriff had touched him.

The Sheriff went on, "Cast off thy tatters, poor friend. I will clothe thee in velvets if thou wilt enter my service as my chief archer."

"Sir," replied Robin Hood gravely, "thine offer doth please me greatly. But far greater would be my pleasure this day if I myself could hang the knave who hath dishonoured thy match by shooting with an outlaw bow."

"Thou art a loyal man as well as a princely archer," said the Sheriff. "Thou shalt have this pleasure. Let us hie to the gallows with this varlet straightway."

Then Will Stutely was tumbled roughly into a wooden cart, and the procession started across the green to the gallows, which loomed darkly over the town.

And still the forty men who were scattered throughout the crowd watched Robin Hood closely, all the while keeping a hard grip on their bows beneath their cloaks.

Although Will had full trust in his master, he nevertheless grew pale as they reached the place of death. But bravely he spoke to the Sheriff in clear, untrembling words:

"My lord, I will take my death as my master Robin Hood taught me. But ere I die, grant me one boon. Place a sword in my hand, and I will fight all your men — though there be a hundred — until the last drop of blood has left my body."

The crowd cheered his valiant words, but the Sheriff cried out in anger, "No! Thou shalt die by hanging — like the dog thou art. And if my luck holds, then Robin Hood shall swing soon after."

Robin Hood, never far from his greenwood friend, bent his head slightly and murmured, "Never fear, good Will, ye shall be free. Methinks this noose would be better fitted to the Sheriff's fat neck!"

Straightening quickly, Robin cast off the patch
from his right eye and thrust out the sword beneath
his beggar's clothes. Then he cut Will's bonds,
shouting, "Now, my merry men! Now let thine arrows fly!"

At this, forty bows came out from forty cloaks,
and forty arrows pointed at the Sheriff's heart. Of a
sudden, the Sheriff leapt from his horse and hid
himself in the crowd. In a moment, all was madness. Arrows fell thick and fast from every side, and
the Sheriff's men scattered in every direction.

When Robin Hood saw that the way was open to
the greenwood, he gave the signal. With arrows still
flying, the band fell back together, and none of the
Sheriff's men dared penetrate the wall of arrows
they made. And so the outlaws made their way to
the shelter of Sherwood Forest.

It was a triumphant band that assembled under
the wide oak that evening.

Though some still bled from wounds taken in the
fray, they were full of joy as they looked up at the
silver arrow with the golden head that hung from
a leafy bough. And no heart was so filled with gladness as Will Stutely's. More than once that day he
had thought he would never again hear the sweet
songs of the birds flying free in his beloved Sherwood home.

7

How Robin Hood Meets Friar Tuck

Aғтеr the triumphant shooting match, Robin Hood bade his men stay safely within the leafy walls of Sherwood Forest. Warning news had reached the glade — the Sheriff had doubled the number of his men-at-arms, for doubled also was his determination to capture Robin Hood and any of his men. Until time should cool the Sheriff's rage, Robin Hood had no wish to cross his path.

And so fall passed into winter. And after many months the spring flowers bloomed again in Sherwood Forest. The days grew longer and warmed into summer.

Meanwhile the men tarried in the greenwood and

played at every sport, feeling their muscles grow harder and their skills become even greater.

One day, as he watched Little John's arrow strike the centre of a mark four hundred feet distant, Robin Hood laughed and shouted, "Hey-ho, but there is none to match thee in all of England."

"Swallow thy words, good master," Will Stutely said. "I know of another who would turn thy head in amazement, so masterful is he with a bow, a sword, and his mighty fists."

"If there is such a man alive, gladly would I meet him and test the truth of what thou sayest. Tell me who is this marvel and where doth he dwell?" asked Robin.

"He is a friar, and ye can find him at Fountain Abbey. But be wary," warned Will, "for his strength is as great as his cunning."

"I have long been thinking that we need a friar among us," Robin said, only half in jest. "He will bless our feasts and pray for our enemies and keep us from evil ways."

So without further say, Robin Hood made ready for his departure. Upon his head he placed a steel cap, and at his belt he fastened a stout sword of steel which glistened blue in the sunlight. His cloak of Lincoln green hid a fine coat of chain mail.

"Take thy silver horn, good master," said Will Stutely, "for Fountain Abbey is not far distant, and we can run to thine aid if need be."

Robin laughed to see Will's troubled face. "Ye would think this Friar more dangerous than five Sheriffs of Nottingham." Nonetheless, he took the horn.

The way led him through shaded dells and broad pastures. Wild flowers filled the air with a delicate scent and made garlands in the green meadows. Robin whistled merrily as he walked along the banks of a wide stream bordered by tall weeds and ferns swaying gently in the summer breeze.

Suddenly he stopped — hearing voices. Listening to the words, he grew puzzled. For though one man asked a question and the other answered, the two voices seemed very much the same. And not a person did Robin see who could solve the mystery.

Now one voice said, "I say a pasty made with green onions is better by far than one made with meat alone."

And the answering voice, which sounded like the first, said, "Yea, there is truth in what ye say, but green onions or blue onions, a pasty tastes like flour without this dark ale to drink along with it."

68

ROBIN HOOD

"Then have a sip." Robin Hood heard next.

"Verily, I will. And thou must take thy two good hands and plunge them into my pie."

Then there followed a time of silence. "They must be sharing a feast," thought Robin, and his mouth began to water, for it was many an hour since he had last dined.

At that moment a strong gust of wind caused the weeds on the bank to bow low, and what Robin saw made him laugh out loud. For there was one man, and one man only, with a pasty in one hand, ale in the other. To Robin's eyes, he was a merry sight.

He was shaped more like a barrel than a man. A loose brown cloak, made of the rough stuff that friars wear, covered his round frame. His head was round as well, with two chins that bobbled up and down as he gobbled his pasty. The top of his head was as smooth and bare as an egg, and fringed all around with a ring of curly brown hair. The stars in the sky did not twinkle as brightly as his blue eyes. But for all his jolly looks, Robin soon saw that the merry friar was as strong as any man in the outlaw band. His arms were as thick as hams; his shoulders could easily hold a bull; and his hands were twice the size of Robin Hood's own.

Now the friar's large hands were busy grabbing large pieces of the delicious pasty before him.

"Good holy man," Robin called to him. "A moment before, thou wert speaking to the wind and bidding an invisible friend to share thy feast. Now I stand before thee, a mortal and better company than the empty air. So share the remains of thy pasty with me, for in truth I am a hungry man."

No sooner did Robin Hood utter his first words than the friar jumped to his feet, clapped his steel helmet upon his head, and drew out a sword that was as long and as sharp as the weapon Robin himself carried.

"What manner of man art thou to spy upon me at my dinner?" asked the friar.

"Only a traveller seeking adventure on the other side of this stream and wishing a bite of pasty in the noonday sun," answered Robin.

"If it's travel thou wish, one kick of my leg will send thee far. Now begone before I finish this last morsel."

Robin's hunger grew as the last bit of pasty vanished, and so grew his anger.

"By all that is holy," he sputtered in rage, "dost thou, who callest thyself one of God's servants, refuse a hungry man a bite of dinner? Methinks thou art but a false friar, and truly thou art a scoundrel."

"Ah," said the friar thoughtfully. "I see why thou
dost think thus. But if truth be known, the pasty
thou didst see me devour was my first bite of food
in two days. For I have been fasting in the Lord's
name for forty-eight hours, and I could swallow
twenty more of the same. If thy manner had not
been so bold, nor my need for food so great, gladly
would I have shared with thee."

Then did Robin's eyes gleam as he thought of a
way to test this stranger's charity.

"Seeing that thou hast not shared thy worldly
goods, perhaps thou canst aid me another way. My
business takes me across this stream, and surely
thou canst see that the clothes I wear are not fit for
wetting. Wilt thou lend me thy strong back and
carry me across?"

"What!" roared the friar. "Here am I, older in
years and higher in God's favour than the likes of
thee . . . and thou darest ask me to . . ."

Then the friar's eyes twinkled brighter than ever,
and his voice changed from the roar of a lion to the
gentle purring of a cat.

"I am but a humble friar, and so I am humbly at
thy service. Not only will I carry thy whole self
upon my back, but I will bear the weight of thy

good sword as well. Here, let me have thy weapon, and thou shalt cross as light as air."

"Good man," cried Robin, "thou art worthy of thy frock." And he unbuckled his sharp sword and gave it to the friar. The friar bent his broad back, and Robin clambered aboard. And so they set forth into the stream, the friar saying naught as the cold water swirled about his legs.

When they were across, Robin jumped down from the friar's back, saying, "I am beholden to thy kindness, good friend. And now, if thou wilt hand me my sword, I shall bid thee farewell."

"Farewell indeed!" cried the friar. "No need for farewells. Fair play is what I want from thee." And he tilted his round, jolly face and slowly winked an eye.

"Now thou sayest that thine affairs must be tended to in haste," said the friar. "But do think of my business, which is of a holy nature, and on the other side of this stream as well. I must get back from whence I came, and since there is no one here but thee to carry me back, and since by some odd fate I hold two swords in my hand and thou hold-est none, I have no doubt that my bidding shall be done."

"A fox would wear thy holy frock with better

grace than thee!" cried Robin, his temper rising once more.

Then, seeing that harsh words fell into seemingly empty ears, Robin tried sweet words. But the friar stood firm, and there was nothing for Robin to do but bend his back. Just before he stepped into the stream, however, he asked for his sword, saying, "Thou art enough of a load without ten pounds of steel to add to the weight on my back."

"Ah, does the babe desire his toy?" said the friar with a mocking grin. He returned Robin's sword and climbed upon Robin's back.

Now the friar was far heavier for Robin than

Robin had been for the friar. Moreover, the friar rode him as he would a horse, thrusting his large feet into Robin's sides, urging him to go faster.

But the going was slow for Robin. Not only was his burden great, but the stream was strange to him. Slowly he made his way, stumbling and tripping over stones, and stepping into sudden holes. When they reached the middle, Robin stopped and cried to the friar, pretending, for a moment of rest.

In truth he used that moment to work loose the friar's sword from its fastenings. The friar, heartily laughing at his prank upon Robin, neither saw nor felt what was being done. So by the time they

reached the bank and the friar leapt down, Robin
Hood was holding the friar's sword in one hand and
his own in the other.

"Now!" Robin spoke in glee. "What dost thou
say of fate, holy man? The very fate thou spoke of
before now seems to have put two good swords into
my hands. So bend thy back and carry me across,
for my hands are nervous and they itch to make
holes in thee if my request is refused."

"Full of holiness am I," said the friar, "and wish
to remain so — not full of holes, I vow. And seeing that fate has now moved to thy side, I will indeed do thy bidding. But if thou hast one ounce of
trust left, give me my sword. I promise not to use
it except to save my life."

So gleeful was Robin to have tricked the friar this
time that he gave the sword to its owner without
further say. Once more Friar Tuck gathered up his
robes and took Robin upon his back.

On they went, the friar wading in silence and
Robin laughing with every step. When they
reached the middle of the stream where the water
was deepest, the friar suddenly gave a mighty
thrust of his shoulders — and Robin shot off his
back. Down into the water he fell with a great
splash.

"Hot spirits need a cooling-off," cried the friar,

full of pleasure at his prank. He turned and waded to the shore, leaving Robin to splash and sputter in the cold stream.

The sight of the friar shaking with laughter made Robin as mad as a bull stung by a hundred hornets.

"Villain!" shouted Robin. "What little hair is left on thine head will be shaved off by this!" And he lunged at the friar with his sword.

But the friar stood ready with his weapon, and to Robin's dismay, he saw that the friar also wore a coat of chain mail.

Thereupon began a clash of steel, which sounded as if the skies had turned to thunder. Mighty and long was the battle as their brandished swords met and clattered. So fairly matched were the two men that neither did harm to the other. For an hour or more the battle waged, each marveling all the while at the other's skill.

Finally Robin Hood cried out, "Hold! This fighting is useless. As for myself, I must admit that thou art the second best swordsman in all of England."

"Good fellow," cried the friar, dropping his sword, "I was about to echo thy words."

"Only one request I ask of thee," said Robin, "and this my last. Give me leave to blow upon my horn three blasts."

"In truth, that is strange," said the friar, "for I was about to ask thee to let me whistle three times."

Each looked at the other with doubt, as each wondered at the other's request. Then Robin blew upon his silver horn three times. At the same moment the friar put his fingers to his mouth and whistled three times.

From one direction came running a score of men in Lincoln green, their arrows ready to fly. From another direction came a dozen giant dogs, growling and baring their fangs.

Robin Hood's men took aim and let loose their arrows. But the dogs ran this way and that, dodging the missiles skilfully. Then the beasts ran up to the fallen arrows, picked them up in their teeth, and laid them at the friar's feet.

"Call off thy dogs, Friar Tuck," Will Stutely cried, laughing at the scene, "and Robin Hood will call off his men."

"Friar Tuck!" exclaimed Robin Hood in amazement. "Art thou truly Friar Tuck?"

"Robin Hood!" cried the friar in like tone. "Art thou indeed the famous outlaw?"

Then the two men came at each other once more, this time not to fight but to exchange glad embraces.

"Had I known thy name, happily would I have shared my pasty in the first place," said Friar Tuck.

"It was my hunger that drove me to trickery," laughed Robin. "But now that I have found thee, and in truth I was seeking thee, come away with us to Sherwood Forest. We will build thee a hermitage for thyself and thy dogs, and in turn thou shalt keep us from evil ways, pray for our enemies, and bless our feasts. What say ye?"

"Aye, I say, and gladly," Friar Tuck said. "For thy name has been known to me for a long time, and now that I know thee, I am in hearty favour of what I know. No worldly possessions have I to keep me here. If I am needed where thou and thy band dwell, then it is there I shall go."

And that is how the jolly friar became one of Robin Hood's band.

And, dear friends, if you read on, you shall see what part Friar Tuck played in the next adventure of Robin Hood and his bold men.

8

How Robin Hood Saves a Wedding

Friar Tuck had never been happier than he was in the greenwood, serving the needs of Robin Hood and his outlaw band. Oftentimes guests were brought to dine at Sherwood Forest much against their will. More often than not, the guest was a rich man who made his money from robbing poor folk, and so he was made to pay dearly for his supper. At these times Friar Tuck would speak a few holy words as the man was forced to empty his purse into the hands of Robin Hood. And when a new man joined Robin Hood's ranks, the jolly friar would hear the vows that each gave, heart and soul, pledging to be faithful to the code of the outlaw band. Ere long there arose a strange circumstance in which Friar Tuck played a noble role. And of this we now shall hear.

One fine morning Little John and Midge the Miller's son were ambling down the high road in search of a guest to bring back to the forest.

"The goose will soon be browning on the fire," said Midge, "and as everyone knows, a fine goose dinner is worth much — ten gold pieces, I'd say."

"Ten!" roared Little John. "Well thou knowest that there are only a few coins remaining in our coffers. Most of our gold went to help the good Widow Smythe and her poor babes. I'd say a fine goose dinner should fetch a price of fifty gold coins. So let us be ever watchful that there be money in the purse of whomever we ask to dine at our board this night."

And so the two merry men walked on, and though they met all manner of good yeomen and honest farmers, no rich nobleman or fat abbot did they see to bring back to their master.

When they turned the bend in the road, they suddenly heard a song so glorious it would shame the sweetest songbirds in the forest. So wild and wondrous was its tone, and so pure was its sound, that the two friends stopped in awe to listen.

Presently the singer came round the bend. The

sight of him was as wondrous as the song he sang. Atop his golden curls perched a hat of green with a tall peacock plume stuck in the center. His coat was half red, half yellow, all tied with gay ribbons streaming this way and that. In his hands he carried a harp made of polished wood with precious stones set about the edges.

The song he sang was of true love and of a wedding to take place on the morrow. Although the two brawny outlaws, and Little John especially, were not men to be moved by stories of love and wedded bliss, they stood breathless as the minstrel strolled by.

"Alas," Midge said when the stranger had passed and his song could no longer be heard. "Were the purses of minstrels as filled with gold as their voices, this one would have been a likely guest at our board this night."

Little John snapped his fingers, saying, "My head must be made of blocks, and thou mayest rightly call me blockhead! We should have bid him come, albeit he has no purse. Think how our master would have loved his songs. But 'tis too late now. So let us do our duty, and be done with it."

All that day and well into the evening they searched but to no avail.

"There is naught to do but return home," said

Little John when the first star brightened the night sky.

As they were about to turn off the high road, they heard a sobbing sound and, looking further, found the source.

There, lying on the ground, weeping rivulets, was the same minstrel they had heard in the sunlit hours.

But as before he had been full of joy, now everything about him spoke of sorrow.

His golden curls were tangled; his jaunty hat was nowhere to be seen; his gay ribbons were torn and dirty; and his harp had been carelessly thrown to one side.

"Ah, what have we here?" spoke Little John. "Something has happened to our merry songbird to clip his wings."

Hearing voices, the sorry lad sprang up. "What dost thou want with me? If it's money, none do I have. If it's song, never will I sing again, for my voice is as broken as my heart. If ye be foe, take my harp, for I want it not. If ye be friend, leave me be. All I wish for is death."

"Foes we are not," said Little John. "And as friends, never can we pass by one who needs our aid."

"Speak not of death," said Midge, "for we have

a friar who will fast come running to say a prayer over thee."

At this a faint smile appeared on the stranger's pale lips.

"In the greenwood dwell hundreds more of Robin Hood's men who are at thy service. This very moment they are making ready a feast." And Little John licked his lips at the thought. "After thou hast tasted our fat goose and drunk our brown ale to wash the tears from thy throat, perchance thou wilt sing a happier tune."

"Very well," said the stranger. "I will go with thee, for truly I care not where I go. And now that I know that thy master is Robin Hood, do I have a choice whether to go with thee or stay where I am?"

The merry men were already assembled when Little John and Midge brought their guest to the wide oak tree to meet Robin Hood. One glance at the saddened lad told Robin that this was no rich man whose purse he could lighten but a friend in trouble.

"Tell us thy name, good friend, and thy purpose," said Robin Hood gently.

"Allan-a-Dale is my name, and as to my purpose . . . I was . . ." At this, his voice broke and tears filled his eyes.

"I know thy name as a famous singer of songs," said Robin. "And as for thy purpose, it is no matter for the nonce. After thou art well fed and well rested, perchance thy story will come easier."

Then all the men looked to their dinner. So joyous were their stories and jests that Robin Hood saw Allan-a-Dale's eyes begin to brighten.

"Now," said Robin, when the bones of the goose were bare and the barrel of ale stood empty, "any guest who dines with Robin Hood must pay!"

"Thou knowest well that I have nothing save this harp, and thou art welcome to it," said Allan-a-Dale.

"Nay," said Robin Hood. "Thou speakest falsely. Thou hast the voice of a nightingale and a story to tell. Sing thy story then. That is thy payment."

Allan looked at the five score of brawny men about him. Well he knew of what they did to men who defied them. Indeed he had sung their stories in happier days past.

So now he picked up his harp and sadly started strumming upon it. Then softly his song began.

It told of a happy minstrel in love with fair Ellen, the most beautiful maiden in all of England. It told that though they were poor, their love and happiness would be riches aplenty. It sung of wedding plans the minstrel and his lady had made, and how the minstrel had come to the town where she dwelt.

There he was to claim her as his bride and take her
to the church the following day, where they were
to be wed.

And, the song continued, when the minstrel came
to town, he was told that the fair Ellen was to be
wed, yes, that very next day — but not to him! A
rich and powerful knight wanted Ellen for his wife,
and this knight had persuaded Ellen's father that
no better match could be made. Ellen was a good
and dutiful daughter and dared not disobey her
father's wishes, though the knight was elderly and
poor in health and the only man she could ever love
was the minstrel.

And so, Allan sang, love is lost to the poor and only death awaits.

When the last note was sung, not a whisper could be heard and even the strongest men there had tears in their eyes.

"Art thou not the same minstrel the song sings of?" questioned Robin softly.

"Aye," murmured Allan-a-Dale, and his tears started afresh. "Tomorrow would have been my happiest day. Instead it will be my day of mourning, for when Ellen is wed to another she will be lost to me forever."

"Nay!" cried Robin. "Men may speak of how we rob from the rich and give to the poor. But in this instance we will not be robbing anyone. We shall only be taking what in truth is already thine. There will be a wedding tomorrow, never fear! But there may be a few surprised faces in the church. Listen well to my plan."

And as Robin spoke, Allan's spirits lifted, his sorrow changed to joy, and when Robin had finished, Allan began leading the men in gay songs.

Had any good folk been stirring on the high road the next morning, they would have witnessed a strange sight indeed. In the lead was Robin Hood, gaily dressed as a minstrel. Behind him came fat Friar Tuck, huge Little John, and a handsome youth singing ballad after ballad in a voice that would have melted the hardest stone. Then followed a score of stout men in Lincoln green, polished bows slung over their shoulders and quivers filled with sharp arrows.

Past rolling fields and up and down little hills they walked, on their way to the town of Plyetree where the wedding was to take place.

When the steeple of the church came into view, Robin halted. "Friar Tuck," he said, "by the best cunning thou knowest, get thyself into the church and hide there till thou dost hear my signal. Little John, take Allan-a-Dale and hide nearby. Keep him from bursting into song until the time is ripe. And all the rest of ye good men, hide among the trees till ye are called for."

And so they did as Robin Hood bade them do.

Robin Hood watched Friar Tuck knock upon the door of the church. A moment later the door opened, and Robin could hear the friar telling an ancient churchman that he was a wandering holy man wishing for a holy place to pray. Then the door closed behind him. The first part of the plan had worked!

Robin Hood watched the road closely, and very soon he saw what he had been waiting for.

A stately procession was slowly making its way

down the high road. To Robin's eyes it looked more like a funeral procession than a gathering assembled for a wedding. Where were the happy faces? The spirited talk? Even the slow-gaited horses seemed in no hurry to get to the church. As they came closer, Robin Hood spied Ellen. Lovely she was, as Allan-a-Dale had said she would be. But surely this was no bride! Her cheeks were pale as sand; her lips quivered; and her lovely white hands were tightly clenched about the reins of her golden mare. And the man riding beside her — Could this really be the bridegroom of such a lovely maiden? Tall and thin, he was, with a sour look about him like a spoiled apple. What little hair he had was gray, and it seemed to Robin that he was twice the age of lovely Ellen.

The Bishop, dressed in splendid robes, gave great yawns as though he would rather be spending the day in sleeping. As for the rest of the company, there was not one smile among them.

When they reached the church, Robin sprang from his hiding place so all could see him. He turned three somersaults and landed upright in front of the Bishop. Such a merry sight was he, so handsome and gaily clad, that even the old knight began to smile.

Prancing about the Bishop, Robin sang:

> Ho for a pretty ballad,
> Ho for a tender song,
> With me at thy wedding
> Naught can go wrong.

"What is thy business?" asked the Bishop impatiently. "Out of our way, lad. We have important matters to perform inside."

"My business is happiness." Robin laughed. "I am a minstrel, at thy service. Folk say that when I pluck my harp and sing my songs on a wedding day, the bride will love the man she marries until the day she dies."

"Love the man she marries, eh?" said the Bishop to himself. "Methinks there is need of thy service here this day. For the climate of this wedding is wintry, though the day be full summer."

To Robin he said, "What is thy price?"

"A purse of gold, my lord," said Robin. "But I will wait for it till the bride and groom are wed."

"Pay it, I pray," cried out a sorrowful-looking man standing close to the bride.

Robin quickly guessed that he was Ellen's father. For the man had such a saddened and a guilty look upon his face it seemed as if he were already sorry for the match he had forced upon his daughter.

"Enough of this," said the Bishop. "Let us begin!" And he was the first to enter the church. Looking helplessly about, the unhappy bride slowly followed, and all the company filed in.

Inside, the Bishop gruffly gave orders as to who should stand here and who should sit there. Then, looking up to where the organ stood, he shouted, "We are ready. Play!"

No one in the church would ever forget the music that came from the organ that day, for who was the organist but jolly Friar Tuck! He struck more wrong notes than would a mouse running up and down the keyboard! Robin had to turn round to hide his smiles. Twitters of laughter came from the guests, but the Bishop, already out of temper, said not a word. Instead he opened his thick book to begin the ceremony.

Then bold Robin ran up the aisle and, forcing his way between Ellen and the knight, cried out in a ringing voice, "Stop! Marriages are supposed to be made in heaven, but this wedding seems like devil's work!"

In the silence that followed, Ellen's glad sigh was clearly heard.

The Bishop, red in the face, shouted, "What does this mean, thou saucy knave? Thou wast supposed to play and sing."

"If it's music thou wishest, then music thou shalt hear!" And lifting his silver horn to his lips, Robin blew three loud blasts.

In an instant, the church filled with men in Lincoln green, the first being Allan-a-Dale who rushed to his love and took her in his arms.

"Robin Hood!" breathed the Bishop. "I should have known."

"Now then," said Robin, with a broad grin. "We shall have a ceremony more to my liking and, methinks, to the liking of this fair bride and this handsome youth."

Ellen blushed, all smiles, while Allan beamed with joy. Seeing his daughter's happiness, Ellen's father now knew how wrong he had been to choose the old knight for her husband. He stood by the happy pair, ready to give his blessings. As for the knight, all he could manage to say was, "Farewell to all this madness!" and he left the church as fast as his old legs could take him.

But the Bishop, who had been promised a fat fee to perform the ceremony, shouted to Robin, "Move from this place, villain! Or I will see that thou art hanged from the gallows before sunset."

"Quiet!" roared Robin. "Or in place of a wedding there will be a funeral — and it will be yours!" With this, sixty bows strung with sixty arrows appeared from under the cloaks of sixty men in Lincoln green.

Looking up at the balcony, Robin called, "Now, good friar, come down and do thy holy work. Perform this blessed ceremony."

So Friar Tuck joined the two lovers in matrimony. Robin played upon the harp and sang a pretty song. The merry men smiled broadly. Then Robin whispered to the angry Bishop, "Did I not make thee a promise? I said that on this wedding day I would play and sing my song, and the bride would love the man she marries till the day she dies. Thou must keep thy promise as well. I will take thy purse of gold."

"Take my curses instead," cried the Bishop.

"Take death then," said Robin calmly. "I have only to nod my head, and my men will shoot their arrows at thy heart."

The Bishop, clenching his fists in rage and frustration, dropped the purse at Robin's feet, turned about, and ran from the church.

Then a mighty cheer arose from Robin Hood and his merry men.

"Oh, Robin," said Allan, "how can I ever thank thee for all that thou hast done?"

"Thou art a good lad, Allan," said Robin, "and if it would please thee and thy bride, come and dwell in the greenwood and be our singer of songs."

One look at Ellen's face, and Allan knew his answer. "Good master," he said. "No one could be happier than I. Today the fairest miaden in all of England is mine. And now I will have the truest friends a man could wish for. Gladly shall I go with thee, and glad will be the song I sing."

And so indeed they were.

9

How Robin Hood Shoots for the Queen and Wins a Bride

IT WAS FULL SUMMER and the wild flowers were ablossom all over Sherwood Forest, but Robin Hood felt strangely heavy at heart.

The cause of his despair he knew full well. Though he tried to think of other things, his thoughts kept turning to Maid Marian, his childhood sweetheart.

It had been too long since he had last gazed upon her sweet face. Indeed he had not seen her, nor had word of her, since the day he killed the King's deer and was forced to become an outlaw.

And now that Allan-a-Dale's bride brought a certain grace and lightness to the rough forest life, he longed even more deeply for his own true love. So often was he out of sorts and short of temper that his loyal men, who loved him more than life, began to murmur sadly that something was happening to their beloved leader.

One day, as he sprawled listlessly on the warm summer grass, listening to Allan-a-Dale sing and play upon his harp, the sound of horse's hoofs reached his ears. Of a sudden, he leaped to his feet and bade his men look to their bows and arrows.

A moment after, there came into view a milk-white steed carrying upon his back a sight fair to behold. It was a young page who came a-riding in, all clad in rich silks and velvets encrusted with jewels.

It was not his costume that made the band stare so mightily but the youth's frail and delicate appearance, and the white pallor of his skin.

Robin ran up and quickly helped the lad dismount.

"Be ye ill, fair sir," he asked, "and so in need of help that ye have wandered into this hidden place? For it is plain to see from thy garb that thou art in the service of a nobleman or knight, or — perchance — a king, and that therefore thou hast no business here."

The youth trembled as he looked up at Robin Hood's face, but ne'er a word did he say.

"Speak, sir," said Robin, drawing his sword, "or I will be forced to open thy lips with this!"

Still silent, the page drew his sword and, with a charming manner, advanced upon Robin.

"Ho," laughed Robin, his good spirits returning somewhat. "I see by the flourish of thy weapon that thou art truly a man to fear!" And with one stroke, Robin sent the page's sword flying into the air.

With that, he chuckled anew and, turning his back on the page, went to join his men. Then quickly the page picked up his sword, and running after Robin, managed to lightly nick his hand with the point.

Robin was more surprised than hurt. Indeed the wound was so slight that it hardly bled. "Thou mayest look like a delicate flower," he said, "but thy petals have a sharp sting." And he cried out to his men in a stern voice, "Surround this young villain."

Quickly the band formed a ring around the frightened youth. Whereupon he sank to the ground and began to sob.

"There now," said Robin, kneeling in front of him. "Prithee explain this mystery. Who be ye and why have ye come?"

In a small soft voice, the page replied, "I have come from the Queen to seek Robin Hood. She bids me bring him back to London Town."

"The Queen!" cried Robin. With that, he clapped the page on the back with such a hearty blow that the page's handsome cap fell off — and down billowed soft, long curls!

" 'Tis a maiden!" murmured Allan, and all the band fell back.

"Marian!" gasped Robin. "My Marian. Is it truly thou? Surely I dream."

And like a man in sleep, he slowly stretched out his arms to her. With a blissful look upon her face, she came to him.

Then Allan-a-Dale began to sing, and the merry men shouted gleefully, for now they saw why their leader had been so downhearted. One look at the happy pair convinced them that all would be well with Robin again.

After a long while, in which they had much to whisper to each other, Robin announced, "Love this fair maiden and treat her well. Now listen to what she hath to tell ye."

Gone was Marian's shyness as she spoke in firm tone to the outlaw band.

"I bring greetings from good Queen Eleanor. Tales of thy bold feats and great skills have reached her ears, and she would fain meet thy leader, Robin Hood, face to face. Furthermore, she hath a boon to ask of him and will tell him more of this when she sees him. She says that he will come to no harm in his travels and that he will have safe passage back to Sherwood Forest. To pledge her word, she bids me give to Robin Hood this golden ring from off her finger."

Solemnly Robin Hood took the ring, kissed it fervently, and slipped it on his little finger, saying, "I would fain give up my life than fail to do the Queen's bidding. Gladly will I travel to London Town and with me shall go three of my men."

Then eagerly did the merry knaves crowd about their leader, for each would give much to be chosen.

"To be fair," Robin told them, "we shall draw to see who goeth. Marian, my love, ask Ellen to help you pluck fivescore blades of grass. Cut three short pieces, mix them all up, and each man will close his eyes and draw one blade. Whosoever draws the three short grasses will come with me."

With quickened breath, the bold men drew, and no one was happier than Allan-a-Dale, Will Stutely, and Little John.

The others hid their disappointment well and crowded about the three lucky men, to wish them a good journey.

"Make ready then," said Robin. "Don thy finest suits of Lincoln green. As for myself, I shall wear red from head to toe. In my absence, Friar Tuck, take care of matters of the men's souls, and Cook, thou wilt as usual see to the men's stomachs."

Soon they were on their way, and a merry sight they were to behold. Allan-a-Dale played on his harp, and Will Stutely laughed to see Little John trying to dance lightly to the music — all seven tall feet of him.

On the way Maid Marian told Robin that when she heard what had become of him, she travelled to London to the court, and was chosen to be a lady-in-waiting to Queen Eleanor. She told him that when the Queen expressed desire to meet Robin Hood, she had begged the Queen to be allowed to travel alone to Sherwood Forest to make the request.

"Ye have grown lovelier since I saw thee last," said Robin, "and braver as well. The Queen has a favour to ask of me, eh? Well I know what favour I shall ask in return." And he gave Marian a look so filled with love and meaning that the lass blushed a rosy pink.

No one stopped them on the high road, but had anyone tried, Queen Eleanor's ring on Robin's finger would have sped them on their way.

At last, when the day was almost gone, they reached London Town. To Robin and his merry men, the cobblestone streets felt hard and strange, so accustomed were they to the soft grasses of the forest. And the great walls and towers of the city seemed to them a prison, for the only walls they knew were the trees of Sherwood.

" 'Tis good that it hath grown dark," said Marian, "for the Queen wishes no one to catch sight of thee. Come. I know of a secret way through the dungeon."

She led them down dark steps, through narrow passages, and up more than a hundred narrow steps till they reached a small tower room.

"Wait here and I will announce thy presence to the Queen." And with a kiss for Robin, Marian was gone.

It seemed hours before they heard a knock upon the door. Robin opened it to see his love dressed in a silver gown with flowers entwined in her hair.

"Thou art fairer than any maiden in all the world," Robin whispered to her, "but thou wert as beautiful to me when thou wert dressed as the Queen's page."

Maid Marian blushed prettily and bade Robin and his men to come before Queen Eleanor.

If the Queen expected to see rough, ill-mannered outlaw knaves, she was pleasantly surprised. Allan-a-Dale and Robin Hood had the noble bearing and manner of highborn knights, and there was hardly a man in the kingdom who could match the stature and strength of Will Stuteley and Little John.

Robin fell down on his knees before the Queen, saying, "I am thine to command."

The Queen smiled. "Thou art welcome, Robin Hood, and all thy good yeomen. Before I make known my wishes, thou and thy company shall have food and drink."

Then they ate and drank, served royally by the Queen's own pages, until they could no longer take another morsel of the rich food or swallow another sip of wine.

At last the Queen told them why she had summoned them. "Tomorrow is the King's tournament at Finsbury. The most renowned archers in all of England will be shooting, and methinks it will be a merry jest for the King's best bowmen to have competition such as thou and thy men can provide."

"Proudly shall we wear thy colours," said Robin, "And proudly shall we pull our bows to shoot in thine honour."

When the King and Queen took their places upon their purple thrones at Finsbury Fields the next day, they beheld a gay sight.

Ten bright-coloured booths stood at the edge of the green meadow, each booth belonging to a dif-

ferent band of royal archers. The green lawns and
crowded stands were ablaze with colour, for the people dressed in holiday best had come from near and
far.

The laughter and chatter stopped as the royal
herald rode his nut-brown horse across the green
and came to a halt in front of the thrones where sat
King Henry and Queen Eleanor.

Then from out of their tents came the archers,
each band dressed in their own colours. A handsome
sight they made, marching as straight as soldiers in
their ranks.

Then the bugle sounded, and in the silence that
followed, the herald announced the rules and prizes.

Each archer would shoot five arrows at the target
of his own band. The three best from each band
would shoot five arrows again. Then the winner
from each band would shoot three arrows against
the winners of the other bands. And so it would go
until only three winners remained. The best of
them would take first prize — fifty gold coins, a silver bugle set with gold, and ten golden-tipped
white arrows. Second prize would be permission to
shoot a hundred of the fattest stags that roam Dallen Lea. The third and last prize would be two tuns
of the finest Rhenish wine.

Now it was time for the shooting to begin. At first there was a great hubbub among the crowd as each man cried out for his favourite band. But as the contest narrowed to the three best from each band, a silence came over the stands as all eyes followed the path of every arrow.

The judges stood near, carefully noting the mark of each arrow as it hit or missed the target.

When the first part of the tournament ended, ten archers — the best from each band — stood before the King and Queen, taking bows from the cheering crowds. The King was well pleased that one of the best was Tepus from his own company. The loudest cheers were for Tepus, Gilbert of the White Hand, and Clifton of Buckinghamshire — these three being the most renowned in all the land.

Then while fresh targets were placed upon the green and the ten bowmen went back to their tents to rest for the hard moments ahead, the Queen made known her plan.

"My lord," she said to the King. "Be ye so certain that these ten yeomen are the very best archers in thy kingdom?"

The King looked at her in some surprise. "Fair Eleanor," he said, "hast thou not just seen for thyself that this is so? I am amazed at the question."

"Then what say ye to this," she said, with a gleam in her eye. "I know of three archers who can match any three of thine who shoot this day."

The King threw back his head and roared so heartily that those around him looked puzzled. "Ye mean to say that ye can produce this day three archers to match the skill of famed Tepus, or Gilbert, or Clifton, and that I have not heard of them? Surely, my good Queen, ye jest."

"I do not jest, sire, nor do I say ye have not heard of them," said the Queen. "But if I bring them hence to shoot against the three best here and perchance they win, what then?"

The King, still smiling, said, "If what ye say prove true, gladly will I offer to them the prizes for the winners. And furthermore, since my Queen hath taken such a high interest in the sport of men, I will offer ye a man's wager."

"Before I hear it," said the Queen, "I ask one boon. Wilt thou grant my men freedom of thy ways so they may travel whence they please without harm?"

"Now curiosity is burning me like a fever," said the King. "Bring the three hither, and I promise that for forty days they can go where it pleaseth them and they will be safe from danger. Now hear my wager. If thy men win, I will give thee ten tuns of

Rhenish wine, ten tuns of brown ale, and a hundred well-crafted bows with arrows to match."

Now it was the Queen's turn to laugh. "If I were a man, I would give much to win such a wager. I accept thy wager of wine, ale, and shooting things, and to match it, I offer thee forty pounds of my best jewels if thy men win."

"I, in turn, accept thy wager," laughed the King, "though in truth I know not what to do with the jewels once I win them except to give them back to thee."

Then Queen Eleanor turned to Maid Marian and whispered to her. Quickly Marian rose from her seat and left the field.

In the meanwhile, the ten archers, having rested well, returned to shoot. And as the King expected, the three best proved to be Tepus, Gilbert, and Clifton. The crowd roared mightily until the herald appeared and blew upon his bugle, whereupon all grew silent and wondered what they would hear next.

"Let it be known," the herald announced to the hushed crowd, "that three men of the Queen's choosing, who have not yet shot this day, will soon come to shoot against the winners."

The gates at the far side of the green opened, and four men slowly followed Maid Marian across the

meadow and up to the royal box. Three were
dressed in Lincoln green and made a merry sight,
but most eyes were on the handsome yeoman clad
all in scarlet red.

All four bowed humbly before the King and
Queen.

"Arise, good men, and three of ye take these
golden handkerchiefs, as ye shall wear my colours
when ye shoot," said the Queen.

"Who are these four whom thou hast brought
here?" said the King, and he echoed the wonder of
all those present that day.

Now it happened that sitting in the stands near
the royal pair was the Sheriff of Nottingham. At the
sight of his enemies, he jumped to his feet and
shouted out in rage, "Your Majesty, seize these
men! The one in red is none other than the hated
outlaw, Robin Hood. And with him stand the vil-
lains known as Little John, Will Stutely, and Allan-
a-Dale."

"Who gave thee leave to speak?" roared the King,
annoyed at the Sheriff's outburst. But he frowned at
the Queen and said darkly, "Is this true?"

"Aye, my lord, 'tis true," she said, all smiles. "The
Sheriff should know them well, for Robin Hood and
his men have often tricked him. Of this I will tell

thee at a later time, but now ye must remember thy promise. Forty days shall they be free to wander where they choose."

"If I loved thee less," said the King, still frowning, "I would fain show thee the anger in my heart. But never fear. I will keep my promise."

Next he turned to his archers, saying, "Brave lads, the prizes and thy honour are at stake this day. Shoot and win, and thy names will be sung in ballads from this day forth. But shoot and lose, and the prizes shall go to the outlaws!"

Murmurs of excitement went round the stands. Even the Queen felt the strain and asked Maid Marian to fetch her a cool drink to wet her dry lips.

Then the match began. First was Will Stutely, shooting against the famous Tepus. So nervous was Will that he held his bow a trifle too long, and his first arrow failed to hit the target.

"Take heed, my friend," whispered Robin, "Do not be overcareful when next ye shoot."

The King leaned back upon his throne and said to the Queen, "If the rest of the outlaws follow this knave's example, I will have thy jewels."

"Nay," said the Queen softly, "speak no more till Little John and Robin have their chance. Then shall I have wine and ale, and bows and arrows."

Fair was Will Stutely's second shot, and so was
the shot after that, but the three arrows of Tepus all
sped true, and he was proclaimed the victor.

Then came Little John against Clifton of Buckinghamshire. Little John was careful not to make
Will's mistake, and knowing Little John's skill, ye
should not be too surprised to learn that the tall
merry outlaw easily outshot his opponent.

The last match was between Robin Hood and
Gilbert of the White Hand, and the stands were so
quiet that the leaves could be heard rustling in the
soft breezes.

Gilbert took the first shot, and no one had seen
better that day. The next shaft and the next fitted
into the centre of the target. Now each seat was
empty, for everyone rose to his feet to cheer the
champion.

Then Robin Hood looked to his quiver and slowly
picked from it three arrows, saying to Gilbert,
"Mine eyes have never seen such brave shooting.
By rights ye should come to Sherwood Forest and
shoot at better targets than ye can find here in London Town."

And even as he talked, he drew back his bow and
carelessly loosed the string.

Once. Twice. Thrice.

The feathers of his arrows lodged so close together in the very centre of the target that they looked for all the world like one thick shaft.

Then the crowd left the stands and came running down to the field, for even a man half blind could see that Robin Hood had won the day.

The King, offering his arm to his Queen, said, "It saddens me to see the outcome, but I do not give my vows lightly. The prizes are to go to Robin Hood first, then Little John, and last to Tepus. The outlaws shall be free — but for forty days only. Then woe to the Sheriff of Nottingham if he fails to capture Robin Hood and all his men on the forty-first day!"

And these words he repeated to the Sheriff, who turned pale and bit his lips.

The King's archers formed a ring about Robin Hood, and while Allan-a-Dale played upon his harp and danced about in joy, the prizes were called out.

"To Robin Hood goes first prize — fifty gold coins, a silver bugle set with gold, and ten golden-tipped white arrows. To Little John, who shot next best, goes the second prize — that being leave to shoot, whensoever ye wish, a hundred stag that run on Dallen Lea. And last, the third prize to Tepus — two tuns of Rhenish wine."

Then up spoke Robin Hood. "Gladly do I accept

the bugle. It will help me to remember this day as
long as I live. But as for the gold, I have no need
of it, and right gladly do I give it to Gilbert, who
is the very best archer outside of Sherwood Forest."

When the cheers for Robin Hood had died down,
Little John spoke next. "What use have I for the
stags on Dallen Lea, for in our greenwood home run
hundreds more. So let each of the ten bands take
pleasure in shooting at them, and may their arrows
hit their mark!"

Each man there vowed that he had never seen
such merry gallant yeomen as Robin Hood and his
men in Lincoln green.

And so the day ended. The prizes were given, and
given again. But Robin was sure that he had the
best prize any man could hope for. For when he
and his merry men took their leave of London Town,
Maid Marian went with them.

And know then, all ye dear readers, that a wedding took place at Sherwood Forest soon after.

And if ye have not guessed the names of the
lovely bride or the gallant bridegroom, go ask another, for I shall not tell ye.

But this I shall tell ye — the next chapter is our
last, and some say the adventure in it is the very
best one that Robin Hood ever had.

10

How Robin Hood Is Pardoned

For forty days, Robin Hood and his men were free to roam the length and breadth of England as King Henry had promised.

Then came the forty-first day and the forty-second, and in all the days that followed they were free. For the Sheriff of Nottingham, though he tried every trick he knew, still could not capture bold Robin or any of his men.

As the years passed, stories of their daring deeds spread far and wide until there was hardly a soul in all of England who had not heard of Robin Hood and his merry band of outlaws.

In the meanwhile King Henry died and King

Richard took the throne. So brave a fighter was this new King that he became known to all as Richard the Lion-Hearted. As he was so often called out of the country to fight for England, few knew him well, though tales of his courage were told throughout the land. After many years spent fighting in the Holy Land, King Richard returned to England, vowing to make a tour of his kingdom the better to know his subjects.

The tales of Robin Hood that reached his ears were so wondrous that especially did he wish to visit that part of England where the outlaw dwelt. He thought it best to disguise himself and his party so none would know them.

And so it happened that one afternoon the Sheriff of Nottingham, seated comfortably before a roaring fire in his great house, was told that a company of friars from a far-off land wished his audience.

Now the Sheriff was sorely vexed that day, for his latest plan to capture Robin Hood had failed dismally, and so he was low-spirited and short of patience, and had no wish to be disturbed.

"Only for a few minutes will I see them," grumbled the Sheriff, "and if I like not their speech, I shall soon send them on their way."

Seven men were shown into the great hall. One

friar, taller and broader than the others, his face hidden beneath his hood, greeted the Sheriff most courteously, saying, "Forgive us this interruption, but tales of thy generosity are known to us. We have travelled a long distance and have need of rest and some food and drink."

"More important matters have I than to become an innkeeper for every man who passes my door," the Sheriff grumbled. "If it's food and drink ye want, go pray for it. Or better still" — and now he chuckled grimly — "get thee hence to Sherwood Forest. Ye can be sure of a meal there — for a goodly price!"

"Sherwood Forest!" exclaimed the tall friar. "But is that not the home of Robin Hood?"

"Aye," said the Sheriff darkly, "and there is none living more evil than that robber."

"But I have heard tales of his courage and valour and of how he has helped hundreds of poor deserving folk," the friar insisted.

"Ha," growled the Sheriff. "Tell thy tales to the King! As for myself, I know what I know. And this I know full well — if ye have any gold hidden in thy cloaks, and if ye keep travelling west till ye reach the woods at the edge of Nottingham Town, ye will find robbers aplenty who will quickly rid

ye of thy last coin. Go beg of them a meal. I want no more of ye. Begone!"

So the holy men took their leave, and the tallest one vowed he would long remember how badly he had been received by the Sheriff of Nottingham.

Mounting their steeds, they proceeded westerly, and any who passed thought nothing of what they saw, except that these were a band of friars bound for some mission or other. When they were deep in the woods, the tall friar drew his steed to a halt and said to the others, "I bid ye, stay hidden among the trees till I summon ye with a whistle."

At that the others protested, saying that their only reason for being was to protect his life. But the friar was not to be persuaded. "Good fellows," he said, "trust me. I think it best I go alone."

So the lone friar went deeper and deeper into the woods, looking neither to the right nor the left, but keeping his eyes straight ahead without fear. Of a sudden he heard the snapping of twigs, and out from behind a thick bush peered the merriest face the friar had ever looked upon.

In a moment the stranger burst from the bush and stepped in front of the friar's horse. Taking hold of the reins, he said with a twinkle in his eye, "Hold, good brother. Tell me thy business in this forest. For it is not often that a stranger passes by these parts without purpose."

"I have lost my way," the friar said, "and I am in need of food and drink, for far have I travelled this day. But I fear these woods for I have been told that they are the home of the villainous robber, Robin Hood!"

Forthwith the stranger dropped the reins and said with a scowl, "Food and drink can I provide ye with. But not before ye take back thy cowardly words. I know Robin Hood better than any man living and I know him not to be what ye call him. Gladly will I take arms against ye to defend his honour."

The friar laughed but kept his mount. "Forsooth, erase thy frown. I like thee better with a smile. As for my words, gladly will I forget them. They are no more than the echo of the Sheriff of Nottingham who hath recently turned me from his door."

At this the yeoman laughed, saying, "If ye be enemy of the Sheriff, then ye be friend of mine." And taking a bugle from under his cloak, he lifted it to his lips, blowing three sturdy notes. In an instant there came running twoscore bold men, dressed in Lincoln green, their bows drawn tight.

"No need for shooting yet," laughed Robin Hood, for indeed it was he. "This friar I chanced upon spoke none too well of me, so fain would I give him three hours to sing a different tune. He also desires food and drink, and since we set a festive table, let him pay dearly for his appetite."

And turning to the friar, Robin said, "Show me the weight of thy purse."

"Pray, good sir," said the friar. "Have ye no charity for a man dressed in holy garb?"

Robin laughed again and said, "Rich friars such as thyself get their wealth from poor gentle folk. We lead a simple life in the greenwood and are beholden to no man. Furthermore we can put thy gold to better use than ever ye can. Drop thy purse, or my men will strip thee of thy frock to find it."

The band of outlaws took a step closer to where the friar sat upon his horse. Then, with a shrug of his broad shoulders, the friar dropped his purse.

"Count the contents of it," Robin said, "to see what kind of feast we shall bestow upon our guest."

Will Stutely and Allan-a-Dale quickly counted the coins. "A hundred pounds, good master," said Will.

"With so much gold, we will not only feast thee

like a king, but entertain ye as well," said Robin.
"Give him back half his gold. Let him not say that
Robin Hood is greedy."

And turning to the friar, he said. "Pull back thy
hood so I can see what manner of man ye be."

"Nay, that I cannot do," answered the friar, "for
I have made holy vows not to show my face for
twenty-four hours."

"Then tell me thy name," said Robin Hood
kindly, for he had taken an immediate liking to this
tall friar.

"Men call me by many names, but thou mayest
call me Father Richard," the friar said gently.

"Richard?" asked Robin. "Ye bear a kingly name,
one that is truly honoured by me and my men.
Huzzah then for this Richard and for our beloved
King, Richard the Lion-Hearted."

Whereupon the merry men gave such hearty
cheers that the friar could not help but smile.

Then, with some leading and some following, the
friar had a jolly escort to the greenwood home of
Robin Hood and his men.

There the friar looked upon a goodly sight as a
hundred men and more bustled to and fro involved
in cheerful occupation, all without apparent command. Some were lighting great fires; others were

turning venison and juicy fowl upon the spits. Wood was gathered and chopped; fruit was picked, washed, and laid upon the table. Not a man was idle.

The friar looked with approval at all he saw. Then turning to Allan-a-Dale, he said in a low voice, "Never have I seen men work so well or so willingly. Is this truly the rough, villainous band of outlaws I have heard so much about? If there is a secret to it, I pray thee, tell me."

Allan looked thoughtful. After a long pause, he said, "I know no secret, and while I have not pondered upon the question before, I see why ye do wonder. 'Tis a hard life we live here, though some would disagree; and if we did not work together, we would not survive. Also it is our leader, Robin Hood himself, methinks. Since no man is forced into this life and each man here trusts and loves him so well, all his rules are followed willingly."

The friar nodded and thought to himself, "I doubt that even the King could command more loyalty from his men than does Robin from his."

Then the friar went up to Robin and said, "I have a boon to ask of thee. Six men of my party are hidden in the woods outside the glade. Methinks by now they are near starving."

"Say no more," said Robin. "Fifty pounds would feed fifty men," And he called a score of men about him and bade them bring the friar's friends hither.

Soon afterward, the six men rode into the clearing, and when they were assured that no harm had befallen the tall friar, they joined the outlaws in preparations for the feast.

And such a feast it was! There was pheasant and fish, roast goose and venison, and freshly baked bread for all. Great tankards of ale were passed back and forth, and the friars in brown ate and drank as heartily and with as much merriment as the men in green.

Then Robin called for the fires to be made higher, the better to see the entertainment that was to follow.

The friar saw stout wrestling matches and bouts of quarterstaff, the likes of which he had never before witnessed. And loud were the cheers for each display of skill.

"Methinks the King himself would be pleased to have in his service the fivescore bold men I see here this day," said the friar to Robin Hood.

"Good monk," said Robin Hood, "there is not a man here in Sherwood Forest who would not willingly let the last drop of blood flow from his body

for such a just and honest king as Richard the Lion-
Hearted."

"Methinks the King would be somewhat surprised to hear such words from the mouth of England's most famous outlaw," laughed the friar. "But
surprised or not, most certain would be his pleasure
to see thy men shoot their arrows, for in truth there
is not a man in England who hath not heard of thy
wondrous skill at that sport."

Then Robin issued a command for the marks to
be set up, and straightway the men ran to do their
master's bidding.

Two garlands of leaves were placed upon the
trees, fivescore paces distant, so far that the friar
had to peer closely to see them.

Robin explained the rules of their sport.

"Each man shoots three arrows. If any man misses
any of his arrows, then he shall receive a buffet from
the mighty hand of Friar Tuck."

First to shoot was Midge the Miller's son, and all
three of his arrows shot straight through. Then came
Little John and after him Will Stutely, and both
men shot full fair, to the resounding cheers of the
friar and his men. Then up came Allan-a-Dale and
— alack! — one of his arrows missed the mark by
a hair.

"A buffet! A buffet!" roared the men and the tall friar marvelled at the good grace of all.

Then Allan-a-Dale stood before Friar Tuck and said, "Strike away, Tuck, but remember how ye love my singing. Save my voice, at least."

Friar Tuck rolled up his sleeve to expose an arm bulging with might and main. He swung and, WHACK, struck Allan's head with the palm of his hand. Down went Allan-a-Dale, arolling and asprawling on the ground, and it was many a minute before he could sit up straight.

The outlaw band roared with laughter, and the friar laughed so hard that tears fell from his eyes.

Then the rest of the band shot in turn, and while most escaped the buffeting, some felt the force of Friar Tuck's hand.

"I see that thy men have all the skill that is sung in ballads," said the tall stranger. "It only remains for thee to shoot."

Robin took his place, and all were still as he shot his first arrow and then his next, which lodged on the mark, no more than a fraction of an inch from the first.

Then Robin fit his third arrow to his bow, and lo! it was badly feathered and missed the mark by an inch!

Never before had the men seen their master miss a mark, and loud was their laughter. But Robin was vexed and said, "Give me five more arrows and I will shoot each one without fault. That arrow had a crooked feather, and 'tis not fair to give me the buffeting."

"Aye, but it was thee who made the rules," said the tall friar, and all about shouted that this was so.

"Very well," said Robin, "but since my missing any mark is rare, let the one who doles out the punishment be rare as well. Good brother," he said to the friar, "let thy holy hand give me my blow."

And without a word, as all sat hushed about the fires as silent as snow, the tall friar extended his arm and fetched Robin such a stunning blow that all who saw it gasped in wonder. As for Robin, he was thrown some yards distant onto the ground, and it was a full three minutes before he could open his eyes.

When he did, he saw as handsome and as strong a face as ever he beheld, for while smiting the blow, the hood had fallen from the friar's face.

Robin shook his head. Had the blow caused him to lose his senses? Surely this was no churchman! Then from here and there came a murmur, a shout,

a roar — "The King! The King! 'Tis Richard the
Lion-Hearted."

And with that, each man there fell to his knees
before the King.

After a moment the King said, "Arise, good fellows, and have no fear."

"Mercy!" cried Friar Tuck, and soft were the
echoes as all called mercy.

Then did the King look stern, and he summoned
Robin Hood to stand before him.

"Thee and thy men are in no danger. 'Tis true ye
are outlaws, and 'tis true ye kill the deer that by
rights belong to me. But haven't ye feasted the King
on his very own food? And haven't ye shown me
greater kindness this day than did the Sheriff of
Nottingham? Right pleased am I to see such a band
of goodly men. And now — to test the truth of what
ye hath said no more than an hour ago — that every
last man of ye would willingly die for the King."

"The King! The King!" shouted all the merry
men. "Long live the King!"

"Ye have heard the truth," said Robin Hood
humbly, and he bowed low to kiss the hem of the
King's cloak.

"Then I give ye all pardon from this day hence,"
said the King.

So great were the cheers that followed, that even the birds awoke to sing along.

Robin cried out, "I swear to thee that every man in Lincoln green stands ready to do thy bidding."

The King looked at Robin's face and was silent a moment. Then he said, "Let thee and threescore of thy stoutest men come with me to London Town to give thy service to me. Let the rest stay here in Sherwood Forest, no longer to pull their bows against my deer but to protect them in the King's name. Pick one of thy choosing, Robin Hood, who is wise of head and fair of heart, for he shall take the Sheriff of Nottingham's place this day."

Cheer followed cheer until each man could shout no more.

As the sun began to wane and shadows crept over Sherwood Forest, Allan-a-Dale sang one last song which seemed to come from the heaven itself, so full of beauty it was. For it told of the life they had known and loved so well.

Robin Hood moved quietly to the King's side and whispered, "Gladly will I leave Sherwood Forest to serve thee, but grant me one boon if it pleaseth thee."

"Tell me of it," said the King.

"Will ye give me leave, some day when I grow old, to come back to these beloved woods?"

"Aye, and more will I give thee," answered the King. "Ye have only to tell me that life in London Town is not to thy liking, and ye may return here."

And so we come to the end of our tale of Robin Hood in Sherwood Forest. As for the days and years that followed, who can rightly say? For some think Robin was happy in the King's service, and others say he yearned for Sherwood.

Some say, that on nights when the moon is round, three clear notes can be heard echoing from the greenwood.

What do ye say, dear reader?